"'Sales is the life-blood of the company.' Thi [...] *quote associated with the no-nonsense world* [...] *any company in any industry.* Peak Perfor[...] for Sales *is a book by sales professionals for* [...] *filled with no-nonsense advice that will keep your mindset open, steady, and clear of anything that keeps side-tracking you from your mission-directive of exceeding sales goals. If you are in sales, this book is for you."*

—ROLANDO GARCIA, III,
Author of *Intrinsic Excellence*

"Peak Performance: Mindset Tools for Sales *is an outstanding collection of sales advice from experienced professionals across the globe. This book provides practical mindset strategies, frameworks, and techniques to help anyone excel in sales. By tapping into multiple perspectives, this book delivers comprehensive insights to unlock your full potential. If you want to boost performance, close more deals, and live a life of purpose on purpose,* Peak Performance *is a must-read!"*

—TONY MARTIGNETTI, Chief Inspiration Officer,
Inspired Purpose Partners, Bestselling Author,
Podcast Host, and Keynote Speaker

*"For those who want to feel good about selling and be successful at selling—*Peak Performance: Mindset Tools for Sales *is the book for you. This book presents readers with multiple perspectives on how to approach sales that feels good and helps you go from having a prospect to getting a buyer. You'll learn things like how to go from presenting to having conversations, how to use active and connected listening with your prospective buyers, and how to sell by telling stories that connect. The mind-shifts about selling in this book are eye-opening. After reading this book, you'll never look at selling the same way. It is an invaluable resource with a variety of insights around sales that will leave you feeling inspired to take your selling journey to the next level."*

—RUCHA BHATT, Life Coach; Co-author of
Peak Performance: Mindset Tools for Entrepreneurs

"Peak Performance: Mindset Tools for Sales *will take the top off of your potential by helping you apply strategies proven to work in real-life settings. You will be compelled to prioritize outstanding customer service, embrace EQ (Emotional Intelligence), and overcome procrastination through applied discipline. This book reveals the secrets to putting customers first, sharpening your interpersonal skills, and staying laser-focused on your goals. With practical advice given through real-world scenarios, it's your guide to becoming a high achiever in all aspects of life. Redefine success and unleash your true potential with 'Peak Performance.'"*

—LARRY MEDLER, JR,
Los Angeles-based Realtor

"Sales—you love it, you hate it (and those might both happen all within one day!). We are all selling ourselves every day, whether it is a product, a service, or yourself and your idea. Peak Performance: Mindset Tools for Sales *is an amazing resource filled with stories, lessons, and actionable tools to take your sales journey to the next level. Featuring 24 different experts on areas of sales, you are sure to find yourself within one, or more, of their stories and walk away with the inspiration and tools to be successful. This book is a must read for sales professionals!*

—JULIE MENDEN, Speaker, Author,
Coach on Leadership & Peak Performance

PEAK PERFORMANCE

PEAK PERFORMANCE

Mindset Tools for
SALES

Authored by:
Erik Seversen, Katie Armentrout, Mike Bosworth, David Brownlee, Heidi Dugan, Shawn Fechter, Karl Gorman, Matt Harris, Wendy Holtz, Florian Hoppen, Loren Kell, Jarvis Leverson, Adrian Logan, Bryan McDonald, Brooke Oliphant, Michel Privé, Laetitia Ribier-Costa, Tim Robertson, Richard-Løvehjerte Rosendahl, Adam P. Smith, David Snyder, Garry Terhune, Désirée van der Laan, Sandra Venere, Amy Wullenweber

THIN LEAF PRESS | LOS ANGELES

Peak Performance: Mindset Tools for Sales individual chapters. Copyright © 2023 by Katie Armentrout, Mike Bosworth, David Brownlee, Heidi Dugan, Shawn Fechter, Karl Gorman, Matt Harris, Wendy Holtz, Florian Hoppen, Loren Kell, Jarvis Leverson, Adrian Logan, Bryan McDonald, Brooke Oliphant, Michel Privé, Laetitia Ribier-Costa, Tim Robertson, Richard-Løvehjerte Rosendahl, Adam P. Smith, David Snyder, Garry Terhune, Désirée van der Laan, Sandra Venere, Amy Wullenweber

Disclaimer—The advice, guidelines, and all suggested material in this book is given in the spirit of information with no claims to any particular guaranteed outcomes. This book does not replace professional consultation. Anyone deciding to add physical or mental exercises to their life should reach out to a licensed medical doctor, therapist or consultant before following any of the advice in this book. The authors, publisher, editor, and organizers do not assume and hereby disclaim any liability to any party for any loss, damage, or disruption caused by anything written in this book.

Library of Congress Cataloging-in-Publication Data
Names: Seversen, Erik, Author, et al.
Title: *Peak Performance: Mindset Tools for Sales*
LCCN: 2023916054

ISBN 978-1-953183-32-3 (hardcover) | 978-1-953183-31-6 (paperback)
ISBN 978-1-953183-30-9 (eBook) | 978-1-953183-33-0 (audiobook)
Sales, Business, Economics, Professional Development
Cover Design: 100 Covers
Interior Design: Formatted Books
Editor: Nancy Pile
Thin Leaf Press
Los Angeles

THIN
LEAF

Thank you for reading this book. There are tools found within the following pages that can greatly benefit your life, but don't stop there. Make sure you get the most you can from this book and reach out directly to the expert-authors who want to help you reach your goals by performing at peak levels as a salesperson and to manifest success in your life. Contact information for each author is found at the end of their respective chapter.

To the pioneers in sales who inspire and motivate us and to those who embrace making the world a better place by providing valuable products and services to customers around the world.

CONTENTS

INTRODUCTION

by Erik Seversen
Author of *Ordinary to Extraordinary* and *Explore*
Los Angeles, California

I was about five years old when I first made money from sales. I grew some carrots and onions in a field by my house, cleaned them up, and put them in a bucket by the road with a sign that said, "5¢ each." One of the first people to drive by was my neighbor who bought all of them for two bucks. I was ecstatic. Then, I was 13 when I actually registered my first business. I sold a book, called *The Hundredth Monkey,* through mail order. Basically, I bought the books in bulk for $0.75 each and sold them for $2.00 each.

While I'm super proud of those two early sales jobs, neither of them was actually a sales job. The vegetable deal was really more of a transaction than a sale. And, selling the books was me buying a few lines of text in the want ads for a few big newspapers. In neither circumstance did I have to convince anyone to buy my product. I was mainly a facilitator of transactions, not a salesperson. There is a difference.

In my mind, a sales job is an extremely precise practice by a professional in their field. I'm not saying a salesperson needs to be an expert at the start, but to be accurately called a salesperson requires looking at sales as a skill just like welding, medicine, law, or engineering are skills that must be learned before great success can occur. Having said that, one of the benefits of the sales profession is that there are often fewer hoops to jump through to become successful. No medical residency is necessary, and there is no bar exam required to work (and excel) in sales. I know many seven-figure salespeople who have very little formal education, but they are great at what they do.

I've been in many conversations with people who argued that there is a particular personality that salespeople must possess to be successful. While I think there are certain personality types that make sales easier, I think sales is a skill that anyone can learn and master if they seriously want to.

I also think sales is one of the toughest jobs out there, and that is why there aren't a ton of top-notch salespeople. Truly great salespeople are very rare, and I think this is partly because of their ability to accept rejection (over and over) without losing momentum. I also think the best salespeople are in true alignment with their values and thrive by helping others find and acquire products and services that will benefit them.

Simply put, I think successful salespeople are incredible, and I admire them.

Recently, my 18-year-old son, on summer break before beginning university, mentioned that he had an online interview for a sales job. While speaking with him about it, I learned that it was a position whereby after some training (which I made sure he didn't have to pay for), he'd have to reach out and create his own leads, and he'd get $27 per appointment he set for a demonstration of a kitchen product. If he actually sold the product, he'd also get a small commission from the sale.

My immediate reaction was to tell my son how hard sales is and that he shouldn't waste his time on this, but I resisted. I thought one of three things would happen. One, he'd get distracted quickly and move on to the next hustle for gas money (like pulling stumps out of my yard for a few bucks). Two, he'd realize how seriously hard it is to make cold calls and actually get people to make appointments (let alone answer the phone), and he'd quit after a few frustrating weeks. Three, he'd sit down, make a plan of attack, and stick with it, quickly forgetting rejections, working harder, smarter, and faster until he was able to actually make relationships with people, gain their trust, and provide a product that would be valuable to them. If this third scenario transpires, I think it could be the start of an amazing life of wealth and freedom if he chooses that path.

I wanted to give my son some sales advice, but I'm not in the category of those whom I consider an expert at sales. Other than a few goal-setting and motivational tips, I couldn't offer much help for sales. However, I know quite a few people who are masters at sales. They are not only good at it, they love it, and they have created amazing lives by using their skill at selling. I think the advice from these individuals would be valuable to my son, who is just starting out, but also to anyone in sales who wants to be better at what they do—who wants to use sales as their method of attaining financial success and personal freedom.

Who are these people? Well, many of them are authors of this book.

In order to create the best book possible, I solicited the help of 24 sales experts from various backgrounds and locations. Since there is no one-size-fits-all prescription for peak performance in sales, the experts in this book come from all over the USA, Canada, the United Kingdom, Norway, Portugal, Switzerland, Costa Rica, and China.

The authors are professionals who are leadership, emotional intelligence, and communication experts, senior business executives, sales coaches, TV personalities, TEDx speakers, LinkedIn Learning teachers, neuro-linguistic programming practitioners, C-suite strategists, commercial real estate developers, and more. The one thing these individuals have in common is that they all have an idea about peak performance, and these ideas can be applied to any situation in sales and in life. These ideas are available to you now.

Although this book is organized around the united theme of mindset and peak performance for sales, each of the chapters is totally stand-alone. The chapters in the book can be read in any order. I encourage you to look through the table of contents and begin wherever you want. However, I urge you to read all the chapters because, as a whole, they provide a great array of perspectives. Each is valuable in helping you tap into your full potential by adding peak performance strategies to your work and life.

It is my hope that you discover something in this book that helps take your performance to the next level, so you can enthusiastically complete daily tasks at work and rapidly reach your goals.

About the Author

Erik Seversen is on a mission to inspire people. He holds a master's degree in anthropology and is a certified practitioner of neuro-linguistic programming. Erik draws from his years of teaching at the university level and years of real-life experience to motivate people to take action, creating extreme success in business and in life.

Erik is an author of 11 books, keynote speaker, adventurer, entrepreneur, and educator who has traveled to 95 countries and all 50 states in the USA. His travels and intersections with people have been a deep study of love, struggle, and ways of thinking that Erik relies on to tackle challenges in school, business, and life. His most current ambitions are sharing the lessons he's learned with others and climbing mountains. Erik lives in Los Angeles with his wife and two teenage boys.

Email: Erik@ErikSeversen.com
Website: www.ErikSeversen.com
LinkedIn: https://www.linkedin.com/in/erikseversen

CHAPTER ONE

SEPARATE YOURSELF WITH STELLAR CUSTOMER SERVICE

By Katie Armentrout
CEO, Sales & Customer Experience Expert
Cincinnati, Ohio

People will forget what you said, they'll forget what you did,
but people will never forget how you made them feel.
—Maya Angelou

She rushed into our store from the hot August sun and made a beeline for the customer service desk that I occupied.

"I bought them like this," the woman said, handing me a deformed stick of wax still shrink-wrapped with the label and our price tag still stuck to it.

"Oh," I responded, trying to maintain a neutral and kind look on my fifteen-year-old face. I'm an expressive person and emotions tend to go straight from my heart to my face without stopping at my brain for filtering. "When did you purchase them?"

"Last week," she replied with an edge to her voice. I didn't know why she was getting impatient with me so quickly when she was obviously lying about purchasing melted candles from us. "They have your price tag on them, so clearly I purchased them here. Honestly, I expect higher quality from you guys. These candlesticks are part of a wedding gift," she lectured me.

"I see," I replied, taking a quick breath. "Do you have a receipt?" After all, it was 1995—a solid decade before technology would allow us to look up purchases on credit cards or email receipts. Paper receipts were the only form of truth and one precious copy existed. Lose your paper receipt and you put yourself at the mercy of the clerk's mood and the length of the checkout line behind you that day. Paper was the only system we had, and it was one that certainly favored the planners, the hoarders, or those who carry a large purse.

"Listen, kid, I clearly bought them here," she said with a rising tone and not even attempting to look for a receipt. I recognized the merchandise and our price tag, but there was no way she purchased melted candles from us. No one would have stocked those on the shelf in that condition. Dad would've fired any person stocking such damaged items.

"Yes, you definitely purchased them here. I recognize the brand and our label. Please excuse me for a moment while I check with our manager in the back." I silently congratulated myself for maintaining composure in front of such a rude customer. My mom's words rang through my head, "Never argue with a customer."

Exiting the customer service desk at a controlled pace, I walked calmly into the office to find my dad. My parents owned the retail gift store that my grandfather started in 1944. We proudly served Dubuque, Iowa, and its surrounding area with gifts and collectibles. Yes, my college education was funded by Precious Moments, Yankee Candles, and Beanie Babies.

"Dad! There's a rude woman who claimed she bought melted candles from us. No one would stock these in the showroom looking like this! And even if someone did, the candles are so deformed that she had to notice their condition and wouldn't have bought them in the first place. Why would she buy deformed candles just to return them? And she doesn't even have a receipt!" I ended my rant to take a breath and ensure I kept my voice down so other customers and employees couldn't hear.

To my surprise, Dad just smiled and shook his head. "Katie," he started in a familiar tone, "the customer is always right. Even when they're not."

"But, Dad," I interrupted him, "she's lying. She probably bought them months ago and left them in her car during the 100-degree weather. No wonder they melted! Why can't she just admit it? They aren't that expensive. We should tell her to spend ten dollars to buy new ones since she messed up."

"Yes, she forgot about them and is upset that they melted. It's unlikely she purchased them like that, but it doesn't matter because the merchandise clearly came from our store. Those candles cost me about two dollars each, so it's not worth arguing with her or asking her to buy new ones. Instead, we're going to invest our cost of two dollars to keep a loyal customer happy," he said.

"Go back to her and *kindly* say that we would be happy to replace the candles for her. Walk her back to the candle aisle, pick out new ones, and show her the Waterford crystal candlestick holders that are a popular gift," he continued. "Invite her to look around and tell her that we'll hold the candles up front, and she can pick them up when she's finished shopping. She will walk away happy and tell her friends that she received great service. A happy customer tells one person, but an unhappy one tells ten. It costs so little to turn the situation around, so make her happy."

Sure enough, she bought the crystal candlestick holders and a few other items that brought her total bill to $68. I even gift-wrapped everything for free.

Why has this story stuck with me for nearly 30 years? My teenage self only saw the customer's lie, but my dad saw an opportunity to distinguish our store from every other place in town. Reflecting on this now, my parents' store wasn't successful because of what we sold, it was successful because of how we made people feel.

Stand Out with Stellar Customer Service

Customer service feels like a lost art these days. We actively use technology to program people out of our lives. We create apps instead of conversations. We prioritize internet connection over human connection. In a world flooded with companies and choices, it is more important than ever to differentiate yourself from the competition.

There's also a new flood of salespeople in today's workforce: the solopreneurs and entrepreneurs who have entered the market. According to the US Census Bureau, there were approximately 4.4 million new business applications in 2020, a 24 percent increase from 2019, with a similar increase in 2021.

While these entrepreneurs are courageous, scrappy, and experts in their field, they also need to be high-performing salespeople to keep their businesses afloat. Coaching isn't limited to sports anymore. You can find a personal coach for anything now like nutrition, exercise, business, finance, mindset, fashion, and life itself. While the coaches are passionate about their topic, very few have sales experience or are even comfortable with the idea of selling. They are lawyers, doctors, teachers, yoga instructors, and ex-corporate professionals who are tired of organizational hierarchy and commuting. They long for a life of freedom and an unlimited salary, which only comes to those who can sell.

Salespeople, solopreneurs, and entrepreneurs are a dime a dozen. A flooded market of salespeople and entrepreneurs isn't all bad because the economy is also flooded with opportunity. But how do you make yourself stand out? If you fall into any of these categories, the best way to separate yourself from the rest is to provide stellar customer service because treating people well never goes out of style.

Here are five principles of stellar customer service

1. Service is not about being right.
2. Solve the problem. Always.
3. Go above and beyond.
4. Create customer-centric policies.
5. Use your voice.

Service Is Not About Being Right

The most powerful lesson I learned in the candlestick story is that customer service is not about being right, it's about how you make people feel. As Maya Angelou once said, "People will never forget how you made them feel." Do your clients feel good about doing business with you?

As a teenager at the time, all I cared about was the truth. The truth was that the customer made a mistake and lied about it to get a free product. If all you care about with your clients is being "right," then you'll miss the bigger picture in business. We are all human and all make mistakes. Customer service goes beyond selling and enters the realm of serving. Serving another person involves humbling yourself to provide value. Selling is a short-term win, but service blooms into long-term loyalty. Customer loyalty is the most fulfilling and profitable place to be.

Solve the Problem—Always

Another lesson my parents taught me was, "Never argue with a customer." Ever. Why? Because arguing doesn't solve the problem. My job as a salesperson is to understand the problem that needs to be solved and work with the customer and my company to solve it. Details don't matter as much as you think they do.

In the candlestick story, it didn't matter how the candles melted or even that the customer lied about it. As my dad said, she was likely lying because she was upset with herself and not with us. His guidance to extend her grace instead of punishment was a hundred percent correct. Especially since it cost the company so little to do the right thing. Sure, it would've been nice if she had told us the truth and asked for a free replacement, but I now understand she was embarrassed and assumed there was no way that we would do that since she was "at fault."

That's the thing about grace, which is defined as "underserved favor." Extending her grace in the situation, even though she wasn't telling the truth, made her feel seen and cared for by us. She would have been relieved to get free replacements, but we went above and beyond to make her feel welcome in our store and assist her with additional shopping needs.

Go Above and Beyond

Not only did we take the damaged product back and replace it at no charge to her, but I escorted her to the candle aisle, picked up new candles for her, suggested complementary merchandise, and invited her to shop further at her leisure. What could have been a negative brand experience turned into a very positive one, and I'm not just talking about her feelings. We could've said no, accused her of lying, and let her walk out angry, so we didn't "lose" money in the transaction. If we had gone this route, we would've lost more than our cost of two dollars per candle, we would've lost her loyalty, which is worth so much more than a few candlesticks. I'm thankful that my parents taught me about customer-centric policies at such a young age.

Create Customer-Centric Policies

A pet peeve of mine is charging customers petty fees for things that are part of the normal customer experience, not an enhancement to it. An obvious example of this is airlines charging customers a fee to check or carry on baggage. When people travel, nearly a hundred percent bring a bag. It's not an "extra" or value-added service, it's an expected customer behavior. Not bringing a bag when you travel is nearly impossible, and airlines know this, so they started charging customers for this service to increase their profit.

As a business leader who's run a profitable P&L statement, I understand the cost of doing business and the importance of profitability. I'm not saying to ignore the cost or not pass it on to the customer, but build it into your profit margin and present a single, all-inclusive price. Or create value-added, optional services that people will pay for like upgraded meals or in-flight entertainment. Customer-centric policies beat company-centric fees every single time.

Consider the "why" behind your policies. Are the fees, charges, and policies customer-focused or internally-focused? Are you enhancing the customer experience or merely finding ways to make more money? Strive for policies, fees, and experiences that meet both your internal needs and those of your customers.

Use Your Voice

Use your voice. Your actual voice. Pick up the phone and talk with someone via voice or video, not text.

According to Dr. Albert Mehrabian, who developed the Mehrabian Method of Communication, only seven percent of communication relies on the words we use and 93 percent relies on non-verbal cues. Our tone of voice accounts for 38 percent and body language accounts for 55 percent of non-verbal communication.

In a world of social media feeds and AI, this means only *7 percent of what we want to say gets communicated when we choose text, email, or chat*. The other 93 percent is left up to the recipient's interpretation, mood, and situation. Emojis, memes, and gifs help make the point, but nothing substitutes for human-to-human conversation.

A phone call dramatically increases communication, but still, only 45 percent of what we want to say is received. The only way to fully get your point across with accuracy is face-to-face communication, either in person or via video conference.

Text, email, and chatbots remarkably improve efficiency, but limit this to straightforward questions or people you know well. If you have a sticky situation or a client negotiation, pick up the phone or schedule a video conference if being in the same room isn't possible. Stop going back and forth with clients over email. If you reach the third email and the situation hasn't been resolved, just call them. You will develop a better relationship with the person, which enables a quicker and more satisfying resolution. It's easy to get frustrated with words on a screen from someone you don't know. It's a lot harder to do that when looking at another human across the table.

It All Goes Back to the Candlesticks

Nearly three decades later, I remember the details of the candlestick story because of the lessons it taught me. As I think through my career as an entrepreneur, national sales director, and business leader, applying these principles is what separated me from other salespeople who were better negotiators, had deeper product knowledge, or a more impressive slide deck. Why? Because I built deeper relationships with clients by serving them and showing them grace. People wanted to work with me more than anyone else because they knew I cared about them and not just making a deal. I didn't always win the deal, but when I did, my clients told me that was the deciding factor.

In a world where you can be anything, be kind. Treating people with grace, gratitude, and kindness never goes out of style.

About the Author

Katie Armentrout is the founder and CEO of Armentrout Communications, a company that's reinventing how businesses think about sales and customer experience. She serves her clients as a consultant, trainer, and coach in sales and customer strategy. Katie is an accomplished business leader known for her ability to connect with complete strangers and her gift of making people laugh.

She earned an MBA from the University of North Carolina at Chapel Hill and a BS in business administration from Saint Louis University. She formerly served as a national sales director at Procter & Gamble and a marketing director and board member of ChangingGears, a nonprofit based in Cincinnati. She completed a marathon, century ride, and triathlon for the Leukemia and Lymphoma Society.

Katie lives in Cincinnati, Ohio, with her husband and three kids. Together, they enjoy camping, hiking, the beach, and roller coasters.

Email: katie@katie-armentrout.com
Website: www.katie-armentrout.com
linkedin.com/in/katiearmentrout
facebook.com/katiearmentrout
@katie_armentrout (Instagram)

CHAPTER TWO

THE FUNDAMENTAL SKILL IN SELLING: CONNECTING WITH STRANGERS

By Mike Bosworth
Author, Speaker, Sales Philosopher, Story Seeker
Orcas Island, Washington

The world is not driven by greed. It's driven by envy.
—Charlie Munger

Statistically, 50 percent of all college graduates will have at least one sales position after graduation. Yet, for most recent college graduates, that's the last job they want to tell their mothers they are taking.

Think back to when you were looking for your first job out of school. What if you had asked your mother how she felt about you taking a sales job? If we could have asked your mothers to give us some adjectives to describe salespeople, how would they answer?

Pushy? High pressure? Dishonest? Sleazy? Manipulative?

Why do so many potential buyers and customers (and human beings) distrust salespeople?

A considerable percentage of the general population has had life-to-date unpleasant experiences with salespeople, which causes them to have a public distrust of anyone in a sales role. The actions of a few bad actors have tarnished the entire profession's reputation.

Here are some examples:

- Pressure or manipulation: many people have been victims of high-pressure tactics to convince them to buy something they may not need or want.
- Misleading claims: many people have experienced unmet expectations caused by salespeople making misleading or exaggerated claims about their products or services. In the software business, we used to call this "vaporware."
- Comp plan issues: many salespeople work on commission, meaning their income is directly tied to how much they sell. This can incentivize salespeople to push products or services that may not be in a customer's best interest.
- Lack of transparency: when salespeople are evasive about the pricing, features, or other details of their products or services, most people quickly distrust them.

The Original Sin

When you become a salesperson, you inherit the "original sin" of being a salesperson. When meeting potential buyers for the first time, you are in danger of becoming the emotional victim of all the unpleasant experiences your buyers have had, life-to-date, with other salespeople. Your buyers reveal this by their discovery resistance, making your job as a salesperson a challenge from the starting point.

Behaving "Like a Salesperson"

We all make judgments about people about their behavior. However, what sellers do NOT want to do is behave in a way that reminds their potential customers of their previous unpleasant experiences with salespeople. Examples of those unpleasant experiences include:

- Not preparing ahead of time and just winging it
- Failing to diagnose before they prescribe

- Hearing problems and immediately trying to solve them
- Providing way too much information too soon
- Telling customer that existing choices are all wrong
- Pushing product features that buyers don't understand
- Asking questions on autopilot instead of generating genuine curiosity
- Talking too much during the discovery or closing process
- Making things sound too good to be true
- Telling you how their product works instead of sharing how you might use it to solve a problem, achieve a goal, make money, or save money

Discovery Resistance

Let me remind you that not all salespeople are untrustworthy or unethical. On the contrary, many salespeople work hard to build long-term customer relationships based on honesty and transparency. However, when meeting suspects (strangers) for the first time, a seller's integrity and good intentions are in danger of being misjudged.

When salespeople call on targeted buyers who *should be* interested in what they have to offer, despite their honorable intentions, many salespeople are dismayed by the behavior of their buyers who resist their efforts to get them to open up and discuss the difficulties of their current situations.

Until potential new buyers feel connected with and trust a new seller, that buyer will most likely demonstrate some *discovery resistance.*

Mindsets and Skillsets

People love to buy but hate to feel "sold to." To replace "selling" with buying process facilitation, sellers must learn to shift their mindsets and skillsets.

What if sellers were able to shift their mindsets and skillsets?

- From presentations to conversations
- From active listening to connected listening
- From "handling" objections to tending and reflecting
- From push to pull
- From pitch to influence
- From logic to emotion
- From "facts" to stories

- From telling to asking
- From buyer control to buying process facilitation
- From closing to decision facilitation
- From being the hero to making their customer the hero

Suppose sellers could learn to align their selling behavior with how their prospects like to buy? In that case, buyers will clearly demonstrate, by *their* behavior, that they now trust their new seller enough to answer their discovery questions.

Public Displays of Trust (PDTs)

In most B2B buy cycles, a "suspect" becomes a "prospect" when a new buyer trusts their seller enough to admit pain to that seller. Buyers do not reveal pain to sellers they do not yet trust.

This public display of trust tells a seller their suspect is now over their discovery resistance! When using buyer-oriented pipeline milestones, this opportunity advances from a (S) suspect to a (P) prospect.

I have a new client with everything going for them—well-recruited, highly competent, high-character sellers with years of sales experience. Yet, in 2022, 80 percent of these "qualified on-paper" sellers struggled to meet their sales goals and expectations.

In my opinion, the primary reason for the missed sales 2022 goals was discovery resistance by their potential buyers.

The Cure for Discovery Resistance

A buyer's discovery resistance demonstrates that they do not trust the seller well enough to answer discovery questions—no matter how well-written they are! But there is a cure—the **power of story**.

Today's sellers are learning to use the power of story to eliminate the discovery resistance *before* they get out their list of discovery questions. Human creatures have used the power of stories for the past 100,000-plus years. Long before written language, stories have been used to pass on tribal knowledge and used by leaders to motivate people to do difficult things that needed to be done.

Today, intelligent parents get their very young children hooked on anticipating and enjoying stories. Parents use story anticipation to motivate kids to get ready for and get into bed! Once in bed, most stories begin with "Once upon a time." Adults anticipate and enjoy stories too. They have watched the brains of adults in MRI machines when they anticipate a story. The critical left brain deactivates, and the right brain opens up (channeling our five senses and feelings).

When adults anticipate a story, they experience a paradox of feelings. On the one hand, they can say to themselves, "Oh, a story! I don't have to *do* anything; I can relax and enjoy." But, on the other hand, their adult unconscious brain tells them, "This might be important information you might have to remember, so you had better pay attention." What a great state of mind for sellers to leverage!

Peer Curiosity

Professional peer curiosity is a powerful feeling in most professional adults, and the initial buying step of most B2B buyers. Imagine I met you at a trade show and your badge told me you are a CISO (chief information security officer). If I said to you, "Oh, you are a CISO! Can I share a quick story with you about a CISO I have been working with for the past 18 months?" the odds are about 99 percent that you would say yes. In ten seconds, I get you (a stranger) to grant me 60 seconds of story time. You are now anticipating a story about one of your CISO peers.

What if I could tell you that story conversationally in 60 seconds?

What if that story had a "setting" where I introduced your peer character to you—background, key resume details, type of organization, and a funny detail about her?

What if that story had the professional *struggle* of your peer? Struggle with C-level execs displeased with her (for reasons that your product directly addresses)—negative business impact of the problem, security risks, and pressures she faces daily?

What if that story had a scenario where your peer (my customer hero) discovered 18 months ago that your organization could give her the capabilities she needed to fix her problems? That she decided to give your organization a shot at helping her become a hero?

What if that story had current business metrics around her successful use of your technology? And some emotional benefit too—more time with family, potential promotion, etc.?

Peer Curiosity to Peer Envy

When you share a 60-second (max) peer story, at its end, you then transition the conversation to the other person with something like, "Enough about me—what's going on with you?"

Your well-constructed peer story led this stranger to some profound emotional conclusions! Emotional conclusions like: "This person understands how hard my job is. This person has already helped one of my peers solve a problem I haven't yet solved. They seem genuine and haven't triggered my memories of other sleazy salespeople."

How do you know? Because if the story is good, they will respond by talking openly and freely. They might even tell you they have been struggling with the same problem. Openly sharing with you demonstrates that this buyer's discovery resistance is gone.

Once you eliminate discovery resistance, you have earned the right to use your expert discovery questions. Once your buyer demonstrates their trust by admitting their pain *to* you, you will still have the regular activities you need to close this business. In addition, you will get to play doctor by building a "buying vision" in your prospect's mind where they can "see" their future-improved ability to respond to their problem by using your offering.

Admitting pain to a seller is a *huge* "public display of trust" by a potential buyer. In my world, that moment is when my new acquaintance of a few minutes converts right before my eyes from a "suspect" to a "prospect"—a *big* event in most CRM systems.

Peer Envy

Let me conclude with an opinion (mine) that **peer envy** is a compelling emotional buying reason in the B2B enterprise sales world. Yes, your buyer will still need proof you can deliver on their buying vision. Yes, your buyer will still need to volunteer to give you access to the remaining silo heads on the buying committee. Yes, you will still have to negotiate and control the proposal process. Etc., etc.

Most people make *emotional* decisions for *logical* reasons. Peer envy gives B2B buyers the emotional fuel to slog through long, complex enterprise buying cycles. Using carefully crafted and practiced "customer hero" stories will enable you to convert peer curiosity to peer envy.

About the Author

Mike Bosworth has been a thought leader within the field of sales over the last several decades. He is an author, speaker, sales philosopher, and story seeker. He is the best-selling author of *Solution Selling: Creating Buyers in Difficult Selling Markets* (McGraw-Hill, 1993), co-author of *Customer Centric Selling* (McGraw-Hill, 2003), and co-author of *What Great Salespeople Do: The Science of Selling Through Emotional Connection and The Power of Story* (McGraw-Hill, 2012).

Mike Bosworth began his career in the information technology industry in 1972 as an application support person for Xerox Computer Services. He was their top new business salesperson in 1975, managed the "Branch of the Year" in 1979, and was promoted to national manager of field sales in 1980.

From 1976 through 1982, Mike designed and delivered sales training programs for Xerox's computer services division. His years of field experience, plus the knowledge he gained from working with Neil Rackham on the Xerox SPIN selling pilot project, inspired him to found Solution Selling in 1983 with a mission to lift the bottom 80 percent. Solution Selling became one of the most widely adopted "intelligent discovery" methodologies in the technology industry. Mike exited Solution Selling in 1999.

In 2008, Mike realized that there was still a "missing link" in understanding why such a small percentage of sellers generate such a large percentage of revenue. Mike's interest and research into how the very best sales professionals connect and build trust with buyers led him to build a framework around how to connect with, inspire, and influence others. Mike founded Mike Bosworth Leadership in January 2013 to begin training salespeople and leaders in using the power of storytelling and story tending for establishing emotional connection, gaining trust, and influencing without authority.

Mike has a degree in business management and marketing from California State Polytechnic University.

In addition to his keynote speaking for professional associations and major corporations, he has been a featured lecturer at the Stanford Graduate School of Business, The Stanford Program on Market Strategy for Technology-Based Companies, The American Marketing Association Customer Message Management Forums, The Anderson School of Management At UCLA, the

Paul Merage School of Business at UC Irvine, The University of Connecticut, and Rollins College, to name a few.

Email(s): mtbent@gmail.com
mike@weconcile.com
Website(s): www.storyseekers.us
www.weconcile.com
LinkedIn: https://www.linkedin.com/in/mikebosworth/

CHAPTER THREE

THE 5 KEYS TO STOP SELLING AND START SERVING

By David Brownlee
Founder, The Brownlee Group; LinkedIn Learning Instructor
San Diego, California

A customer is the most important visitor on our premises. He is not dependent on us. We are dependent on him… We are not doing him a favor by serving him. He is doing us a favor by giving us an opportunity to do so.
—Mahatma Gandhi

February 15, 2008, my life changed forever. My wife and I were in the capital of Nicaragua, Managua, trying out a new sushi restaurant with friends. We heard it was amazing and we wanted to see it for ourselves. It was awesome. The sushi was flown in fresh, the atmosphere was contemporary, and the service was top-notch. After dinner, we went outside to grab a cab to bring us back to our hotel. During our five-minute cab ride back to the hotel, the driver stopped and two people jumped in. One in the front seat and one in the backseat with my wife and me. Then it happened—the guy in the front seat pulled out a handgun, pointed it at my face, and demanded money. In my shock, I grabbed his gun, but his partner in the backseat pulled out a knife. He grazed my midsection with it before shoving it into my right thigh. When he pulled it out, blood shot everywhere. The guy with the gun pistol whipped me in the face and head. I thought we were going to die.

As weird as it may sound, I used everything I had ever learned about sales—influence, persuasion, rapport, etc.—to calm the situation and get us out safely. Luckily, my wife made it through unscathed. In the end, they got 300 dollars, two cell phones, and my wedding ring. At the end of an extremely long walk (as if we were in the final credits to a horror movie), I limped into a hospital, healed up, and now share my story from stage with my new mission—to dedicate my life to helping others.

Most people would characterize what happened as "the worst thing that has happened in your life." I look at it as a gift. This episode gave me a renewed purpose, passion, and fulfillment in my life that I didn't have before. My journey has landed me in this book, here, with you. I believe that you have the power to make a positive difference in our world, one customer and one prospect at a time.

After college I sold tech products for a Fortune 100 company and then helped grow a beverage company and managed sales teams on the West Coast before the company was sold to Pepsi. Throughout my sales career, I have been blessed to sell millions of dollars' worth of products and services. I've had the pleasure now of training over two million people, from small businesses to Fortune 100 companies, and have conducted over 5,000 one-on-one coaching calls with executives and sales professionals. What I've learned is that the old adage, "Nobody likes to be sold, but they all like to buy," is simply not true. What is true is "Nobody likes to be sold, but they all love to be served."

After over 30 years in sales, I came up with an acronym for making more money as a salesperson. It's based on thousands of hours of research, science, and my real-world situations and sales survival. The acronym is BUCKS because we all want to earn the "big bucks" in our businesses and sales careers. Here's how you do it.

B—Be the Expert

In 2013, YouTube was on the rise as a great way to connect with prospects. At the time, I was a business coach and sales consultant. Clients would come into my office for a session on sales process, strategy, etc. My goal was to expand to group coaching online and selling online programs. The problem was, I had zero prospects in my pipeline. It gets worse. I had no credibility in the marketplace. How in the world was I going to attract new clients that knew me, liked me, and trusted me? I was talking with a friend, and he suggested that

I go on YouTube and shoot education videos to establish my credibility. I was skeptical at first, but what did I have to lose? Nothing. I decided to give it a try.

I filmed myself teaching sales, customer service, and marketing. I posted the videos and got horrible results. Then a funny thing happened after about three months. I started to get a little bit of traction. I checked the videos and I had about 100 views each. Then 200, 400, 1,000, 5,000. In a few short months each video had over a hundred thousand views. The customer service video surpassed a million. I had no idea what to expect. One day, I was at the store and I got a phone call. It turned out to be a representative from one of the largest cell phone companies in the world. He told me that he had been training his people from my video for free for so long, it was finally time to pay me. I enthusiastically agreed. He ended up hiring me to come speak to his team and provide live training. This was the beginning of seriously upping my sales game.

The takeaway that I got from this experience is that we all must be an authentic expert in our field. Sharing our knowledge with others is the fastest and easiest way I have found to do that. That helps build likability and trust with your prospects before you ever talk to them. It creates a desire for them to do business with you, the expert.

U—Uncover the Dream

Several years ago, I owned an entertainment and special events company. We provided DJs, bands, lighting, video production—you name it—for special events. One year, we got the chance of a lifetime for our business. One of our prospects was a giant movie studio. We wanted to provide the entertainment for their Academy Awards after-party. The problem was, we were up against bigger companies who had been around longer than us and who had stellar reputations in Hollywood. How could we possibly compete with that? We had already spent a ton of money marketing to the entertainment industry and were running out of money … fast. This was our last chance to make this campaign work and save our business. I needed to come up with a solution ASAP.

That's when I came up with what we called at the time, the "Event Information Sheet." It was a series of questions that I came up with that focused on serving the prospect and helping to make their vision a reality. We didn't look at this process as selling. Rather, we looked at it as serving. I was focused on the client's vision for their party and reviewed these questions with them. Throughout the process, I always took copious notes. When it came time for me to make my pitch, I used everything I could that was already in their vision in order to serve them and turn their dream into an enjoyable event. How did it turn out? I ended up getting the business and many more events from that studio after that. Our competitors were shocked. They couldn't believe that a little company from LA could land such big deals.

I discovered something from this experience that changed my sales career forever. Customers are most concerned about their dreams and visions. Not your product or service.

Here are three things to remember when uncovering your prospect's dream.

First, ask them what their dream or vision is. You may call it a goal, objective, or target as well, depending on the client and the situation. Write down exactly what the prospect tells you, in the exact order they tell it to you. Why? Because 99 percent of the time, they will share with you what is most important to them first, then the next most important thing, etc. Then, repeat their dream to them and ask if there's anything else they would like to add. Capture all the information and repeat the elements of it in the order in which they gave it to you. Be sure to use the same exact language they used so that they feel heard, understood, and cared for by you and your company. It works like magic to gain buy-in from prospective customers.

Next, ask your prospect why their vision or dream is important to them. The "why" behind their vision is the most important aspect of the result they are after. This is where the true decision is made. If you can show that you understand and empathize with their "why" for making this purchase, your chances of success with this prospect go up.

Third, ask your prospect how they would like the process to go in working with you. This is important, because you want to know what your prospect's expectations are of doing business with you. Then, repeat back to them what they expect. Let them know as much as you can what you can accommodate. Share with them how you can help them fulfill their vision and provide them with the results they are looking for.

C—Conquer Challenges

Several years ago, one of the world's largest motorcycle companies reached out to me to help them with a huge project. They were getting ready to launch a new rental and travel department into 300 dealerships across the US and internationally. There were some major problems with this idea.

First, there was no communication between the dealerships and this new program. They were introducing new technology into hundreds of dealerships at once. Team members at each location had never done this before. And to top it off, they were opening a brand-new call center for sales and service in Las Vegas. How could I possibly bring all this together into a cohesive system that got them the results they were after?

They told me that their goal was to hit a 25 percent increase in revenue year over year in the next 12 months. So, what should I do?

First, I did a keynote to build excitement for what was to come. They were having their annual dealership summit in Las Vegas. They had already heard about what was coming and were not excited about it. The keynote changed that.

Next, I conducted on-site sales and customer service trainings. That helped them understand how they could sell the dream to their customers and help take care of them during the hiccups that would arise during the rollout.

Finally, we implemented a monthly group coaching call with their team to address the challenges they were facing during the rollout and throughout the year.

After 12 months, we hit their goal. Very few people on the team thought that we could do it.

The takeaway is to always help your prospects overcome their challenges. Call out the challenges they face now and the challenges to come. Then, show proof of how you can solve them. Remember, in order to make a sale you have to uncover what their challenge is. Otherwise, there is no urgency for the prospect to get the deal done. That's when you end up waiting and waiting for a decision to be made and eventually lose contact with that prospect.

K—Keep Following Up

Early in my consulting career I was prospecting for clients—because I didn't have any. I researched my ideal client and made a dream list. One of the companies on my list was an online athletic company looking for sales training. I reached out to them, but they never responded. They didn't respond to my emails, my phone calls, or my ESP (extra sensory perception) trying to will them to answer me. I was getting frustrated because I knew they would be a great client. So, one day, I went on Facebook and found the HR person's profile. A funny thing happened. I came across an engagement video that she and her fiancé had shot. They announced that they were getting married in a tiny Italian city in the Italian Riviera called Amalfi. It had a beautiful church with 80 steps leading up to the entrance. It was one of the most beautiful churches I have ever seen. That wasn't the coolest part. The coolest part was that my wife and I got married in the very same church! So, how could I use this commonality to possibly help me make a sale?

I picked up the phone and called her again. Needless to say, she didn't pick up, so I left a voicemail. I told her, "I think we have something in common. I got married at a beautiful church in Amalfi. I'm thinking maybe you did too. That's so cool! Hopefully we'll get a chance to talk about it soon."

You'll never believe what happened next. She called me about five minutes later, screaming with excitement on the phone. "I can't believe you got married there too! Isn't it a magical place? Oh my God! This is amazing!" she exclaimed. Right away we booked an appointment to meet at her office. We did have a great conversation about getting married in Italy, visiting Positano and taking a boat to explore and shop on the Island of Capri. It was an awesome sales call. In fact, I got offered a job as a sales trainer. But for me, I was looking for consulting work, so it didn't work out.

In the end, I did not bring them on as a client, but it was a great teaching moment for me in my sales career. We all know that we should always follow up with our prospects. The research says we should expect to follow up 12 to 15 times before we get the opportunity to make a sale. What this experience taught me was not only do you need to follow up, you must be creative in your efforts.

S—Stuff Your Pipeline

I recently got a call from an organic farm to help them with their sales training. They had a decent-size team, and they wanted me to develop a sales process, training materials, and SOP for their sales department. They had a goal to grow exponentially this year. For me, it was a six-figure contract for a couple months' worth of work. It was a decent deal for a small business like ours. So, I went through their legal department, jumped through hoops and did everything I could to put together a great pitch presentation and contract. I'm pretty good at this, so I was looking forward to kicking off the project.

Then it happened. I didn't understand that this was actually happening to me. They "ghosted" me. They stopped responding to my emails, texts, phone calls, and my famous ESP techniques. Nothing. Radio silence.

Up until that point, we had been talking, emailing, and texting almost every day. Even on weekends in putting the project together. I started my traditional follow up, but this felt different. I consulted with my team and the consensus was that this was not our ideal client. If a client is going to ghost you during the discovery and contracting phase, if they become a client, they could be a nightmare to communicate with and partner with to get them their desired result. We took that into consideration, but I continued to follow up anyway.

In the meantime, I reached out to other companies in my pipeline that were looking for dates that work for their training. Through this process I found another company that was happy to take their slot. They paid the same amount of money over the two-month period, and it was a company that was much easier to work with. We were ecstatic.

Through my follow-up process, I eventually did get through to the CEO again. Of course, she told me she was busy and I should call back. The jury is still out on whether or not we should work with this client. We'll find out in the future.

The key lesson in this story could change your sales success for the rest of your career. Always have another prospect ready to fill the slots you have available to sell. Having a full pipeline takes the pressure off of you as a salesperson. I have a friend who is one of the best insurance salespeople in the country. He hits his sales quota for the year before the end of Q2. He created so much free time for himself he decided to take up golf. Now, he spends his time golfing with his largest clients and lives the most stress-free high-performing sales professional life I have ever witnessed. All because he keeps his pipeline full of his dream prospects. I believe that you can do the same.

BUCKS

Let's review the five steps that will allow you to serve instead of sell. If you want the big bucks, here's how to make it work for you.

First, be the expert. Build your personal brand as a salesperson. Make sure you're on social media, writing articles, shooting videos, or simply sharing industry articles of value with your prospects

Second, uncover the dream. Make sure that with every prospect you are uncovering their dream or vision. Do your best to find out why that dream or vision is important to them. Uncover how they envision the process of doing business with you. Your customers are most concerned about their dreams and vision, not your product or service.

Third, conquer challenges—your prospects' challenges. Make sure that you find out what your prospects' challenges are. Find out what effect those challenges will have if they don't find a solution. What effect it will have on their company, on their revenue, or even on them personally. Introduce your solution to their challenges and prove that your solution actually works. Present case studies, testimonials, success stories, or even referrals.

Fourth, keep following up creatively. Follow up via email, phone, and social media. Look for commonalities or something personal to the decision maker that you are trying to connect with. Have fun and dedicate the time consistently to uncover ways to creatively connect with your dream client. In the beginning, it may feel like a waste of time. If it's the right client, it won't be.

Fifth, stuff your pipeline. Calculate how many people you could serve in a 12-month period. Strive to fill your pipeline with the highest number possible to fulfill your quota one month or one quarter at a time. Fill your pipeline with the end number. The largest number you can. This will give you time and stress relief, and give you the ability to walk away from unworthy clients. Remember to use all five steps and serve instead of sell. You got this!

About the Author

David Brownlee is a customer experience, communication, and leadership expert. He is the CEO of The Brownlee Group, LLC and founder of the Rockstar Customer Service Training Program. He is a two-time, number one best-selling author of *Rockstar Service, Rockstar Profits*, and *Customer Service Success*, and has been featured in Time Magazine, People Magazine, and others.

David is a former business coach and seminar leader for Tony Robbins and has conducted over 5,000 one-on-one coaching sessions with business owners and executives. He has trained over two million businesses and individuals from his online courses, keynotes, live events, and coaching programs. His clients range from small businesses to Fortune 100 Companies—from Harley-Davidson and Oakley to Google and LinkedIn.

David currently lives in San Diego, California, with his wife and two children.

Fun fact: David is the biggest winner in the history of the Hollywood Squares Game Show on CBS with Whoopi Goldberg.

Want more FREE resources to optimize your sales process? Go to www.davidbrownlee.com/bucks to download your FREE *Bucks Action Guide,* a customizable PDF that will help you close more business and serve more clients.

Website: www.DavidBrownlee.com
LinkedIn: www.LinkedIn.com/in/brownlee

CHAPTER FOUR

SIMPLE STRATEGIES TO TAKE YOUR SALES FROM AVERAGE TO AMAZING

By Heidi Dugan
Celebrity TV Host, China Market Expert
Shanghai, China

Everyone lives by selling something.
—Robert Louis Stevenson

I firmly believe that the act of selling has unnecessarily become something that 1) instills fear in people and 2) is perceived negatively. During my younger years, I pursued acting and discovered that mastering the art of selling oneself is undeniably one of the most vital skills to acquire. Sales is not solely the domain of salespeople, rather it is something that everyone will need to do at some point in their life, normally many times. Whether it involves presenting ourselves in an interview, pitching an idea, or persuading others, these situations all involve the essence of selling. Once we grasp this concept, selling becomes an exhilarating prospect, as we realize its potential to profoundly impact our life, career, and the people around us.

What exactly is sales? Sales is very simple, but it is far more than a mere transaction. It embodies the art of effectively conveying an idea, a product, a thought, a project, or a proposal in a way that convinces others to TAKE ACTION.

Consider this: at some point in everyone's life, there will arise a time where you will need to sell something. Whether it's selling yourself during a job interview, pitching an idea to a friend, promoting a product or service to a customer, or even selling a vision to investors, sales permeates our daily existence. It serves as a vital performance indicator, reflecting our ability to lead, communicate, create purposeful products, influence others, persuade, and genuinely demonstrate care for those around us.

I was very lucky because I learned from a very young age that the better I sold my ideas, the more likely I was able to do the things I wanted. When I was a young girl, my father was quite strict towards my siblings and me. Whenever we wanted to go out with friends or stay up late, he would ask us a question that has stuck with me to this day: "Why should I let you?" Then he'd ask us to write two lists. The first list was all the reasons we thought he should agree with us. The second list was a list of reasons why we didn't think he should agree with us. It may seem strange, but this exercise proved invaluable as it allowed us to anticipate and address any objections he might have.

Little did I realize at the time that this technique would become a recurring tool in my life, particularly in the realm of sales. It evolved into a captivating game for me, where I would challenge myself to generate a long list of potential objections and then skilfully counter them with compelling reasons. This method became instrumental in my ability to persuade others to see the value in my ideas, products, or propositions. Interestingly, I now employ this technique with my own children, recognizing its effectiveness in teaching them how to anticipate objections and present persuasive arguments.

I truly believe learning how to sell is arguably the most important skill you can develop. Whether you love it or not, sales is the one crucial element that can yield results in various aspects of life. I cannot emphasize enough how important it is—for you, your team, your sales department, your PR, your marketing efforts, and even your children—to learn this skill. Mastering the art of selling sets you apart. It's the one common thread among all accomplished individuals.

The beautiful thing about selling is that the best way to do it is through authenticity. Believe in what you say, create situations and products that genuinely help others, and watch the magic unfold. It is not a stomach-churning, fear-filled task that needs to be done. Instead, it becomes a powerful tool to make a positive impact on the world. When you realize that your good ideas, products, or services can genuinely make a difference, selling becomes an avenue to create incredible change and do immense good.

Ultimately, the true measure of success in sales lies in your ability to drive action. When the other person takes action based on your influence, you have successfully completed the sales cycle. And if you've done a good job, they will be happy with their decision and become your raving fan, continuing the selling cycle on your behalf.

Let's now take a look at five proven strategies that will help you supercharge your sales. As a matter of fact, these are the only strategies a person can use in sales. It's important to realize that there are only five ways you can increase your sales. I have worked with hundreds of companies and no matter the company, whether a service provider, a food product, or a beauty product, they all only had these five strategies to take their sales from average to fantastic. Once you know them, they will pave the way for your business's success.

This is how simple sales is. You can:

1. Increase the number of leads
2. Increase the percentage of conversions
3. Increase your prices
4. Increase the average sale or package
5. Increase the number of repeat buys

Ideally you would only work on one area at a time. Once you have optimized that area of your sales, move to the next. They can be done in any order. Let's take a look at the different tactics you can use to optimize each area of sales.

Strategy 1: Expand Your Reach and Increase Your Leads

This area focuses on widening your pool of potential customers. By increasing your leads, you create more opportunities for conversions. Here's how you can make it happen: imagine you run an online clothing store. You could optimize your marketing channels by identifying the platforms that resonate most with your target audience. Whether it's Instagram, TikTok, or email campaigns, make sure to assess who your target market is and where they shop, or what apps they use and like. You could give something away like an e-book that focuses on educating or helping your ideal customer. Make sure this is valuable and represents the standard of product that you will eventually sell to them.

Another effective tactic is to implement lead generation techniques. Offer something valuable, like a style guide or a limited-time discount, in exchange for customers' contact information. Additionally, leverage search engine optimization (SEO) techniques to improve your website's visibility and attract organic traffic.

Strategy 2: Optimize Your Conversion Rate

Converting those leads into paying customers is the next crucial step. It's not just about the quantity of leads; it's also about the quality of your conversion process. Let's explore some tactics to optimize your conversion rate.

Imagine you're a freelance graphic designer. To enhance your website's user experience, make sure it's visually appealing, easy to navigate, and mobile friendly. Streamline the client inquiry process, keep your portfolio up to date, and showcase your most impressive projects. Test different call-to-action buttons and optimize your landing pages to encourage visitors to take that next step and contact you.

Another effective tactic is to leverage social proof. Display testimonials, case studies, and endorsements from satisfied clients on your website and social media platforms. People trust the experiences of others, and positive feedback builds credibility and boosts your chances of conversion.

Strategy 3: Strategically Raise Your Prices

Now, this one might sound a bit counterintuitive, but trust me, it can work wonders for your sales. Raising your prices strategically can position your business as a premium provider and attract customers seeking higher value. Here's how you can go about it.

Let's say you run a specialty coffee shop. Highlight the unique qualities of your coffee beans, the care you put into the brewing process, and the delightful ambiance of your shop. Emphasize the exceptional taste and experience customers will have when they choose your coffee. By effectively communicating the value and differentiation, you can justify a higher price point.

Another approach is to offer tiered pricing or bundled packages. Create different options to cater to various customer segments. Provide additional perks or exclusive features at higher price points to entice customers who seek a more premium experience. Alternatively, bundle your products or services together to offer value and increase the average sale amount.

Strategy 4: Maximize the Value of Each Transaction

Once you have customers interested in making a purchase, it's crucial to make the most of each interaction. By increasing the average sale amount, you can boost your revenue. Let's explore two effective approaches:

Imagine you own a tech store. Implement cross-selling and upselling techniques by recommending related or upgraded products to customers. For example, if someone buys a smartphone, suggest a protective case or additional accessories. Provide incentives like discounts or freebies to encourage customers to add more items to their cart.

Creating limited-time offers can also be highly effective. Promote exclusive deals or bundled packages that provide additional value for a slightly higher price. By creating a sense of urgency and scarcity, you can tap into customers' fear of missing out and motivate them to seize the opportunity and spend more during their current transaction.

Strategy 5: Foster Customer Loyalty for Repeat Business

Building a loyal customer base is like having a goldmine at your fingertips. Encouraging repeat purchases can significantly impact your sales and drive long-term success. Here are two ways to foster customer loyalty.

Imagine you own a local bakery. Providing exceptional customer service should be at the core of your strategy. Greet your customers with a warm smile, engage in friendly conversations, and go the extra mile to make them feel special. Remember their preferences, offer personalized recommendations, and ensure their experience is memorable. By building a strong relationship with your customers, you increase the likelihood of repeat visits.

Another powerful tactic is to implement a customer loyalty program. Offer rewards, discounts, or exclusive perks to customers who consistently choose your business. Whether it's a punch card system for coffee purchases or a tiered membership program with increasing benefits, make sure your customers feel valued and appreciated for their continued support.

By implementing these five proven strategies, you'll be well on your way to increasing your sales and achieving business success. Remember, it's all about expanding your reach, optimizing conversions, strategically raising prices, maximizing transaction value, and fostering customer loyalty.

One last thing—remember to always focus on talking and connecting with your ideal customer. It's very difficult to sell a car to someone who doesn't drive or to convince a person that only has enough money to get by from week to week to buy a 300-dollar skincare product, no matter how much they enjoy looking at your Instagram account. Before you start selling make sure you know exactly who you want to sell to and who can benefit from your product or service. It will make the sales process so much easier and be far more enjoyable as you will be adding real value to someone's life. Helping a busy mum with healthy meal options by selling her quick, easy healthy packaged meals delivered to her home is adding massive value to her and her family's life.

Now it's time to take action! Reflect on your business and identify 1. your ideal customer, 2. which of the five strategies you will first implement. Finally,3. create a plan of action.

Good luck, and here's to your continued success in boosting your sales and reaching new heights in your business journey!

About the Author

Heidi Dugan is a living, breathing and inspiring story of success. An entrepreneur, celebrity TV host, wellness advocate and media darling, are just some of the terms used to describe her. Having lived in China for almost 30 years, Heidi became the first foreign TV host to have her own TV show in China, which reaches over 6 million viewers daily. She is a live host on Oriental Shopping channel, completing up to $2 million in sales in one and a half hours.

Heidi is a highly sought after ambassador and adviser to foreign brands, focusing on health, wellness, beauty, and food and beverage categories, and leverages her experience and influence across a wide range of online and offline platforms.

Heidi has received awards such as Best Foreign TV Host and Most Popular Foreign TV Host, International Leading Woman in Business of the Year, International Alumnus of the Year, and Australia China Alumni Award for the Arts and Creative Industries.

As Director of Arete Group, Heidi offers companies and brands strategic advantage to successfully integrate into the community, connect with the consumer, and ultimately build their business faster in China, one of the largest economic markets in the world.

Her influence across Australia and China has been recognized through her media coverage on Channel 9 news, Australian Financial Review, Harper's Bazaar, China Daily to name a few.

Website: www.Heididugan.com
Linkedin : Heidi-Dugan
Instagram: heidi_dugan
Chinese Official Accounts:
Heidi中洋生活 : Xiao Hong Shu | Douying | Weibo | Wechat

CHAPTER FIVE

INCREASE YOUR SALES CONVERSIONS BY 900%

By Shawn Fechter
Sales, Marketing, and Subscription Executive
Long Beach, California

Opportunities are like sunrises. If you wait too long, you miss them.
—William Arthur Ward

If you grew up in a large family or spent time in the military, the idea that "the first one to the table eats" will instantly resonate with you and bring back memories of the chaos around the dinner table or in the mess hall. If you weren't seated at the dinner table or in line at the mess hall when the food started being served, you very likely weren't leaving with a full belly.

The same can be said for businesses that rely on consumer leads, whether B2B or B2C, that come in over the phone, through a CRM tied to your website, or from organic and paid social media. You would think, especially with the insane cost most companies pay to acquire engaged leads, that it would be a priority to have a plan in place to ensure salespeople are doing everything possible to convert these leads to sales. The reality is that most salespeople and teams are failing miserably at this.

The Five-Minute Rule

Sources, including MIT and insidesales.com, show that responding to a lead within the first five minutes (versus 24 hours) increases your chance of converting that lead to a sale by 900 percent. Yes, you read that correctly—you increase your chances of converting a lead to a sale by 900 percent if you can respond within the first five minutes.

But let's give ourselves a little bit of cushion, right? Five minutes seems a bit insane. According to research published by HubSpot, consumer patience wears out in just ten minutes, citing that 82 percent of consumers rate an immediate response as important or very important when they have a marketing or sales question. What's even more important is that your chances of converting that lead to a sale decrease by almost ten times if your response time drops from five minutes to just ten minutes. Given the critical importance of response time, you would think it would be the number one priority of any company that engages consumers in a sales funnel.

Would it surprise you to learn that recent statistics shared by ServiceBell show that the average response time for most companies is 47 hours? What if I told you that almost 75 percent of leads are never responded to at all? We are talking about the critical importance of responding within five minutes, yet most companies have a response time of two days, if at all. Let me put this in a scenario we can all relate to.

It's a Monday night in October, and like most Monday nights during this time of year, I'm on the couch watching Monday Night Football. My wife, who could care less about sports, is in the bedroom watching *Fifty Shades of Gray* for the 37th time. It's the start of the fourth quarter and my wife just finished *Fifty Shades* and glides around the corner in some new sexy outfit and with that certain look in her eye. I'm a man, and even though we are hardwired to miss signs, there is no mistaking the significance of this look. I tell her I will be there in five minutes. She gives me the standard "don't bullshit me" look, and I reassure her I will be right there. Forty-five minutes later the game is over, and I do my best Magic Mike strut into the bedroom to find her about 40-minutes deep into what would turn out to be a great night's rest for her and a frustrating and costly missed opportunity for me. I had my window, didn't respond within the window of that opportunity, and paid the price.

Consumers today are no different from my wife. They get emotionally attached to a product or service, make the decision to engage a company in the sales process, and wait. The problem for us is that they don't wait very long before moving on to the next company, they completely lose interest because something else now has their full attention, or worse, they think we do not value them as a customer. The latter of which has massive long-term ramifications.

Yes, I know we don't all have an army of sales agents staring at their computers and phones, ready to pounce on every incoming lead within seconds, but I'll get to some ways you can close that time gap in a bit. For now, here comes the next important number: fifty percent of consumers purchase from the first company to respond.

Given the alarming numbers above, the first company to respond to a lead may, in fact, be the only one to respond. If you can't create a customer sales funnel that allows for a five-minute response time, at the very least create one that simply responds.

I was recently hired as a consultant to help map out the lead response plan and customer journey for a growing car rental company. The first step in the process was to create a fake customer persona and assess what I have always felt is the most important aspect of the company's sales funnel and lead response time. I sent a request as "Tom" who was interested in five cars that would each be needed for one week for a corporate event that would happen in a few months' time. I let them know I was hoping to secure everything in the next couple of days, so I could move on with my planning. The results were in line with what I expected. Of the inquiries sent to 50 car rental locations:

- Twenty-nine of the 50 locations responded.
- Twenty-one of the 50 locations never responded.
- Zero responded within the first five minutes.
- Of the 29 responses:
  - Only six attempted a call to the provided phone number.
  - Only two attempted more than a single email response.
  - Only four attempted both a call and an email response.
  - None made more than two attempts to reach me to close the sale.

How do you think the owner and sales leaders of this car rental company responded upon seeing these statistics? How would you respond if this was your business, knowing that more than 40 percent of your locations failed to respond to an urgent request for five weeklong car rentals, as well as the opportunity to secure what could potentially become a long-term corporate client?

You have a 50 percent chance of converting a lead to a sale if you simply respond, yet most companies fail to respond at all. And those that do respond tend to do so long after the emotional attachment to your product or service has worn off, or when the consumer has turned their attention to the million other things they are being bombarded with daily.

Okay, Okay, You Get It. Now What?

Simple, you need a lead response plan that fits within the framework of what your company can realistically implement.

Everybody Has to Buy In to the Importance of Lead Response Time

Sales leads can come at you from all angles today, and many departments or teams may be involved in responding to them. You may have a contact center that handles phone calls, email, and web leads, while your marketing team has a person dedicated to social media posts and interaction. Any potential integration likely involves your technology team, and if you have retail locations, every in-person customer interaction is a lead managed by a team that may flow up through operations. Or your company may be a one-person show. It really doesn't matter if you are a 500-employee company, or if you are running a home-based business from your garage—if you don't get the buy-in on the critical importance of lead response time and the commitment of human and financial resources to perfect it across all channels it, many of your leads will die on the vine. Sure, it might be the hot topic around the leadership table for a few months, but the buy-in from the top down is necessary to move it from rhetoric to it permeating every facet of your company culture.

Start with the Basics

Ensure, at the very least, that you are responding to 100 percent of all incoming leads across all channels. I don't care how good sales are today, statistically even the top-performing companies and sales teams are leaving leads to die on the vine. The easiest way to do this is to make lead response as important an incentive as sales performance for your sales leaders and team members. Your top-performing sales agent may be doing double what the next agent is, but if they leave leads unanswered, they are costing the company money and missing opportunities to earn long-term customers. Make lead response and lead response time as important a measuring stick of sales success as the sales numbers.

Set a maximum lead response time based on what your current staffing and incoming calls, emails, social, and CRM leads will allow. Ideally that is five minutes but draw a hard line in the sand at whatever number is realistic. If it is two hours, then stick to that number like your lives depend on it. If it's 12, 18, 24, or whatever the number, hold your sales leaders and your teams accountable to reach that target, all while working on your plan and timeline to eventually get that number down to five minutes.

Pick Up the Phone!

If a customer sends a lead via any channel and includes their phone number, it is an invitation to call them. Please pick up the phone and call that customer. The odds are they won't answer on the first attempt, as it typically takes up to eight attempts to reach a customer, even when they've submitted a lead. If they do not answer on the first attempt, leave a message and send a text message letting them know who you are and that you are following up on their recent inquiry. The odds are they didn't answer your first call because they didn't recognize the number. Now, set yourself seven reminders in your calendar at intervals of once a day to contact them until you have reached eight attempts or you have been in contact.

Be Relentless with Your Follow-Up

As mentioned above, it can take as many as eight attempts to contact a customer that has submitted a lead. Don't take it personally or as a sign that the customer has moved on if they do not respond after the first or second attempt to reach them. The most likely reason they are not responding right away is that life simply gets in the way. I prefer the "carpet bomb" follow-up approach. This means you hit them across multiple contact points assuming, of course, you have more than an email to work with. If you have a phone number, hit them with a call and text. If you have email, set your Outlook or CRM to send automated follow-up messages at your desired intervals. I'm a big fan of the automated email systems that allow you to place a customer in a defined bucket that determines the frequency and message journey based on their initial inquiry. I would also encourage sales agents to do a bit of research to find the customer on social media and send them a direct message with an invitation to speak. In all correspondence be sure to leave your full name, the hours you can be reached, as well as your direct phone number and email address. I know this seems very basic, but I've worked with sales teams at enough companies over the years to realize that the kiss of death for any sales leader is to take it for granted that the basic rules of sales are being adhered to.

Be Creative

In today's world of chat bots, automated email campaigns, social media, and the countless other communication channels we have available to engage our customers, the most successful companies are the ones that use creativity, keep the mood light, and make the process fun and enjoyable. Think about the endless barrage of promotional emails, social ads, and even text messages you receive from companies each day. Which ones do you typically open? For most consumers, it's the ones that contain fun, lighthearted, and visually appealing content. That content can range from the casual and positive way a salesperson responds to a customer email or web lead, to a stunning image or high-production value video, and everything in between. The goal is to connect the customer on an emotional level to your product or service, and to make your company stand out regardless of whether you have the lowest price or best product compared to your competitors.

Be Authentic and Make It Personal

I have trained sales teams and agents in everything from heavy equipment and timeshare to adventure travel and vehicle rental. The number one thing I try to instill in each of them is the value of an authentic and personal response to each incoming request for information. There is nothing that makes me pull my hair out faster than when I see a salesperson using a copy-and-paste or canned response with a customer in an email or simply reading from their website or a script when speaking on the phone. Sadly, today's consumers are conditioned to expect no response from inquiries they send, and if they do get one, it is usually a poorly constructed, canned version of what they already read on your website or saw in your email blast or social post. The best salespeople understand the value of a personalized response and take the time to treat each email or phone call as if the customer were sitting next to them having a casual conversation.

Know Your Stuff

Customers considering a purchase of 1,500 dollars or more spend an average of eight to 12 hours doing online research prior to their first inquiry. The research time drops a bit as you slide down the purchase price scale, but the point here is that your customers are typically well versed and educated in your product or service before they ever speak with a sales team member. This makes it imperative that salespeople are, at the very least, equally as educated in your product or service as your potential customers are. I have always trained my sales teams to a point where they can be on the phone with a customer and navigate them through purchasing any of our products or services by memory. The best salespeople also know the competition's website and product offerings by memory and can speak confidently about the value in doing business with their company.

Engage Them in the Sales Process

If a customer didn't need to be sold, they would have already purchased your product or service online. They have made the emotional connection, now they just need you to help them make the decision to spend their money with you. Be creative, be authentic, make it personal and fun, know your stuff, and help create a happy, lifelong customer. If you master the ability to be the first one to the table and do all that, you will soar past your competitors and watch your sales numbers explode.

About the Author

Shawn Fechter is a sales, marketing, and subscription executive with an adventure travel company based in Los Angeles, California. Shawn's expertise in relationship-based sales and his commitment to the "5-Minute Rule" have helped him build multi-million-dollar-producing sales teams for his current company, as well as others over his 30-year sales career. Shawn started his career with Hertz and Caterpillar before earning the honor of Number One Salesperson out of more than 100 in the USA for the global power production company Aggreko in 2000 and 2001. Shawn spent ten years in Mexico where he trained and developed sales teams for timeshare and real estate in Puerto Vallarta, Cancun, Playa Del Carmen, and Cabo San Lucas, before moving to Southern California and taking on his current role. Shawn continues to work as a sales trainer to this day. He lives in Long Beach, California, with his wife and two children.

Email: shawnfechter@gmail.com
LinkedIn: https://www.linkedin.com/in/shawn-fechter-6674b957/

CHAPTER SIX

FIVE TRAITS OF A GREAT SALESPERSON

By Karl Gorman
CEO of GLH, LLC, Real Estate Developer
San Diego, California

I am the master of my fate; I am the captain of my soul.
—William Ernest Henley

To be a professional salesperson, you are paid as much as a doctor, lawyer, or other highly trained individual in our society. However, you typically don't go to Harvard or have an MBA from Yale. Most sales professionals, just like me, were not the smartest people in the class but figured out how to get through the courses with good grades.

Salespeople don't always have the highest IQs, but the best always understand how to play the game of life, so we can enjoy high-paying salaries and all that it brings. In this chapter, I am going to tell you exactly how to be a great salesperson to ensure you live the life of comfort or even abundance you desire.

For me, it was a very traumatic experience in college that changed my life and made me want to be a salesperson. Before this experience, I wanted to be a gym teacher and a basketball coach. But after, I knew that having money could potentially help me create an even playing field for life.

I was walking down the street at Michigan State University with three other students who look like me—we are all Black. We were approached by a police officer and asked for our identification. My friends knew what was happening and pushed me to the front of the pack to talk politely to the officer.

"Would you like our school IDs or our drivers' licenses as we all have both?" I said. The police officer replied by saying, "Drivers' licenses." At this point, it was no longer just one officer and his partner; it was four police cars and eight total officers looking at us.

"No problem," I replied and turned to my friends.

"Hey, guys, give me both your student ID and driver's license." Everyone complied.

I handed the officers all of our cards and smiled and said, "Here's both, just in case."

We stood for ten minutes, until the other officers asked us to please be seated on the ground. We now were on the side of the road, in the middle of our university campus, sitting with our arms behind our backs. This went on and on and on as students were passing us the entire time on their way to a campus football game.

Finally, after an hour, the officers came back with our identifications and said, "You guys are free to go."

We all stood up, and one of my friends uttered, "Wait, why were we stopped in the first place?"

Immediately, we were slammed to the ground, and with guns pointed to our heads, one of the cops screamed, "You are going to die tonight, N*****!"

At that moment, my short life flashed before my eyes and changed me forever. In that moment I made a commitment to myself to never be in that situation again. How do you change that moment from never happening again? I can't change the color of my skin as this was obviously racial profiling. I thought hard that night and what I came up with was to change my social status and make as much money as I possibly could.

When arriving on my campus that next Monday, I went straight to the guidance counsel and asked, "How do I make as much money as I can?" The counselor said, "You will either have to be a doctor, lawyer, or business professional."

I knew I couldn't be a doctor. I also had interned with a lawyer and saw how boring that was. So, I asked a few more questions about this business professional.

"You have to be a salesperson," she said. "They make a lot of money and often get a company car."

WHAT? A company car? I had never heard such a thing. "How much do sales professionals make?"

"I don't know exactly but $85K with a company car if you are the best," she said. Well $85K was more than I could imagine. Hell, I was living off of five-dollar pizzas and drinking water from the tap. I changed my major and put my head down to make $85K and drive a company car.

Four years after college, I was making $450K per year and driving a brand-new Lexus! There are five things that I think were key to making this happen—persistence, mental toughness, a high EQ, listening more than speaking, and being genuine. Let's look into these.

Top Five Things That Make a Sales Professional Great

ONE: Persistence

In the realm of sales, persistence is an indispensable quality that separates successful sales professionals from the rest. Persistence is the ability to stay focused, determined, and resilient in the face of obstacles and rejection. Salespeople must understand that a "no" does not necessarily mean a permanent rejection but rather an opportunity to improve and find alternative ways to reach goals.

Persistence involves maintaining a positive mindset and viewing each setback as a stepping stone towards success. Successful salespeople understand that they may encounter numerous rejections before closing a deal, but they view each rejection as a valuable learning experience. By persisting, sales professionals learn to adapt their approach, refine their strategies, and identify new opportunities.

When I started my career at one of the largest insurance companies in the world, I was given a list of people to call and a cubical with a phone. My manager at the time was a great guy and he told me what to say. How was I persistent? One way was that I practiced day and night when I wasn't actually on the phone.

Being persistent isn't something that is often taught, but you can develop it. It's a mindset that no matter what happens, you won't quit. Time and time, hour after hour, I would call the phone numbers trying to get a meeting, and if I actually got someone on the phone, they would tell me they were not interested. And that one nice person that would say, "Okay. Come to my office at 10 am tomorrow." Then when you show up, they are either not there or had canceled before the message got to you.

At the start, I made 25 in-person sales calls a week. In order to get those meetings, I had to call 99 times before getting one person to agree to a face-to-face meeting. You do the math on how many calls that was.

TWO: Mental Toughness

In order to survive in business as a sales professional, you must have toughness between your ears. The person who thinks they will fail and the person who thinks they will succeed are both most likely right.

The way you approach life is 90 percent mental. Sales can be a mentally challenging profession. Salespeople face rejection, deal with setbacks, and encounter high-pressure situations regularly. Therefore, developing mental toughness is crucial for achieving long-term success in sales.

Mental toughness is the ability to stay focused, motivated, and composed, even in the face of adversity. Sales professionals with mental toughness do not allow negativity or setbacks to derail their progress. They maintain a positive mindset, manage stress effectively, and bounce back quickly from disappointments. Developing mental toughness involves cultivating self-awareness, practicing self-care, and embracing a growth mindset. Salespeople should continuously work on their emotional well-being, seek support from mentors or coaches, and engage in activities that help them build resilience and mental fortitude.

I can remember the first "lunch and learn" I set up after calling a firm several times, over and over again. A "lunch and learn" is when you bring in lunch for the entire office, and, while they eat, you give them information about your company. If done successfully, you get the executives from the company in the room for 30 to 45 minutes and you let them know why you and your company are so special.

I was all ready to go with sub sandwiches and pizza for options. I had small bags of chips and cookies for dessert. After weeks of waiting for this day to arrive and having gotten all the food and packets of information to pass out, I was ready to go. I got there early before anyone was in the room. Packets of information were ready at each chair, and the lunches were in the back of the room for everyone to choose from.

Once noon hit, people started to show up. I was so excited and nervous. They filed in, one after the other, and started to grab sandwiches and pizza.

They were talking and cheerful and everything was perfect. After everyone had made their way in and sat down, I was ready to give my 30-minute speech and answer any questions.

"Shall we get started or are we waiting for anyone else?" That was the phrase taught to us to start the meeting. I delivered the line perfectly. One of the executives looked up at me and said, "Where is your boss?"

"My boss is at the office," I replied. He closed his folder and picked up his lunch and walked out. The other executives in the room looked at me and did the same. I had about 30 people in the room and all of them left, one by one just as they'd come in.

"Next time, bring your boss!" one of the executives shouted. No one brought their boss to a "lunch and learn." After driving back to the office, I went directly to my boss's office and convinced him to do a "lunch and learn" with me to give me feedback. He agreed, so I called them back the following week and got another "lunch and learn" scheduled. The lesson is—I didn't stop. I could have let that situation define me or shape me, but it didn't. I was not going to let this firm dictate how I felt about myself or my success in the business. Four years later, this same company was one of the greatest-producing agencies I had in my sales portfolio.

THREE: High EQ

Emotional intelligence (EQ) is defined as the ability to understand and manage your own emotions, as well as recognize and influence the emotions of those around you. The term was first coined in 1990 by researchers John Mayer and Peter Salovey, and was later popularized by psychologist Daniel Goleman.

EQ is really made up of five components starting with self-awareness. This is the ability to recognize and understand your moods and emotions and how they affect others. Next is self-regulation. This involves being able to control your impulses and moods and to think before acting. Next comes internal (or intrinsic) motivation, empathy, and social skills.

It's amazing how the most successful people in this world have really high EQ. Having a high IQ (a standard of measurement used to assess a person's mental aptitude compared to a group of their peers) allows you to solve equations, write books, or develop a movie script. Having a high IQ is extremely important, but my personal opinion is that EQ allows you to be successful with people and your network of people, which is your net worth.

I became aware of my EQ as an adult and realized that not everyone had a high one. I was a sophomore in college when it became apparent. My fraternity hosted a booth the very first day of school with fraternity members looking for the next set of young men who would pledge. People would come up and interact with us. During this, I began to clearly see effective and ineffective communication styles between fraternity members and potential pledges. I made mental notes on what types of communication made people feel welcomed and appreciated, and what type of communication created the opposite effect. At that moment I became aware of my own high EQ and how I could read a room or audience, and alter my energy to make people feel comfortable.

Whether I am presenting in a board room at a Fortune 100 company or walking down the inner city of Detroit, I am comfortable and can make other people comfortable. In sales, one of the most important things to do is make the person you are with as comfortable as possible. Until they get comfortable, they will not trust you or even hear what you have to say. All of us have some insecurity and while we can't always see or feel it, it's there. Until that insecurity is addressed either verbally or non-verbally, you can't get potential buyers to the place where they can make a decision to move forward.

FOUR: Listening More Than Speaking

Most people think you have to be a smooth talker to be in sales. You go back and watch any sales movie—*Glengarry Glen Ross*, *The Wolf of Wall Street*, and *Boiler Room*—are some of my favorites. In these movies, the main character is always a smooth-talking, smooth-dressing, and good-looking guy. And don't get me wrong, it helps if you have some, if not all, of that. However, I have been in sales for 20 years, and I have seen the overweight, small, less-than-attractive salesperson make millions and millions of dollars. How? Simply by listening.

You see, most people (including salespeople) are insecure, and when you meet with them, they want to tell you how great they are and what they have accomplished, the business school they went to, the MBA they have, and the awards they have won. They do this all to be accepted by you. This is where most salespeople, or people in general, make the mistake.

The key in sales is not to fall into the trap of talking too much. Keep it about the person you want to sell something to or who you want to build a relationship with. If the person says, "I went to Northwestern business school and graduated top of my class," don't respond by telling them where you went to school, even if you graduated from the top of your class at Harvard. Rather, just say, "Really? Wow, tell me more about Northwestern." My guess, if they are like 90 percent of the other people in the world, they will go on for another while on the details. And when they stop, ask them another question about it. I have been to lunch or dinner meetings for hours and hours and walked out, and my guest feels like it was the best meeting of their life, and it was because they heard themselves talk during the whole meeting.

By staying curious, asking questions, and listening, you will earn the trust of the person you are meeting with.

FIVE: Being Genuine

The art of being genuine and authentic is not something that can be taught or learned, unless you truly want to engage with other people. On the subject of what makes salespeople successful, you most likely won't learn about being genuine in a sales book, school, or on YouTube video. But I will tell you with everything in my body—this is the most important piece of selling anything. If you are not honest with your buyer, not honest with yourself, or not honest about your company, then this is not the profession for you. If you are not authentic about those things, then it's going to be difficult to sell anything.

When I led the insurance company in sales those first years out of college and was flown to a great location and put up in a five-star hotel, the president of the company asked me to speak at our national convention. He wanted me to talk about what I did to be successful every year.

"What is it, Karl?" he asked. "Is it price, features, and benefits? Or is it our customer service?"

I didn't say this to him, but our price was higher, our product was okay, and our service sucked. "I don't sell price, product, or process. I sell people," I replied. People don't buy what you sell, they buy why you sell it. People buy from me because of me. That's it. People do business with people they like— the true authentic person! I always start my presentation (when I have to talk and can't just listen) with a picture of my wife and kids as they are my focus. From the first few minutes, you know what makes my "why"!

Figure out your "why." Be persistent, have mental toughness, understand your EQ, listen more than you speak, and be genuine. With these things, you too can be wildly successful at selling anything.

About the Author

Karl Gorman is the founder and CEO of GLH LLC, managing partner of Valhalla Capital, cofounder of Black Future Foundation, and board member of The University Club Atop Symphony Towers. Karl has been recognized as among the Top 50 Most Influential Leaders and has over 20 years of corporate American experience where he worked for a few of the largest financial institutions in the world. He is currently working in a $3B international company and running several multiple multi-million-dollar real estate projects. Karl has a beautiful wife, Cheryl, of 15 years and three kids, Grant, Laurel, and Halle.

Email(s): Karl.Gorman@GLHLLC.NET
Karl@VALHALLACAPITAL.IO
LinkedIn: LINKEDIN.COM/IN/KARL-GORMAN-8B291817

CHAPTER SEVEN
DISCIPLINE IS DESTINY

By Matt Harris
Growth Partner, Entrepreneur, Investor
Brighton, England, United Kingdom

Discipline is the bridge between goals and accomplishments.
—Jim Rohn

Simple, relentless discipline is the key to becoming the best version of yourself. To master anything, improve personal performance, and achieve your biggest goals requires discipline. It drives you to take the action necessary for personal growth and success.

I honed in my ideas about discipline as I spent eight years building a commercial cleaning business before selling it, as well as growing a property management business to 100-plus rooms in 18 months before the COVID-19 pandemic shut it down.

Now, I've poured my discipline into running The Growth Lab, a growth partner for cleaning and FM businesses. We help business owners identify growth opportunities through strategic partnerships and by executing a buy and build strategy to increase top-line revenue.

On this roller-coaster ride as a serial entrepreneur, discipline is the key that helps me navigate the ups and downs. With each success or failure, discipline allows me to focus on taking action regardless of feelings or external influences.

In life and business, you need discipline to perform at a high level. It determines whether your achievements are a flash in the pan or a repeatable event. Top sales performers produce the best sales outcomes because they take action. They focus on completing the most important activities every day to hit their goals. This is a major requirement to achieve peak performance as a salesperson.

The Importance of Self Discipline

Discipline is having a mindset and the ability to get things done, no matter what. It's the internal force that drives you to take action and be better. It's the ability to train yourself to behave and work in a routine way and build healthy and productive habits. The most successful people use discipline and deep-seated motivation to achieve their goals.

Starting my cleaning business made me understand the importance of discipline. It also forced me to start a morning routine, which allowed me to quit my "day job" and grow my business. It was discipline that helped me develop habits to set me up for success.

When I started my cleaning business, I was working full-time as a property lawyer. I soon realised that to work on my start-up, I needed to engineer more time while having a demanding job. That's when I decided to wake up earlier and be more intentional about how I began my day. I wanted my business to succeed, and I had an inner drive to take control of my life. I saw quitting my 9-to-5 and running my own business as a means to achieving that. The discipline of waking up at 5 am every day helped me perform the habits that took me closer to my goal.

Being disciplined first thing in the morning also filtered through to the rest of my day. It had a positive impact on both my business and my day job.

In *Discipline Equals Freedom*, Jocko Willink outlines four reasons why you need discipline:

1. **Discipline makes you the master of yourself.** Discipline helps you take control over your thoughts and actions. You overcome bad habits, excuses, and distractions as you carry out the daily tasks that lead to your long-term goals.
2. **Discipline makes you healthier.** By taking control of your actions, you have the power to resist unhealthy temptations. Instead, you develop and maintain habits that keep you healthy—like a good diet and regular exercise.

3. **Discipline helps you reach your goals and realise your full potential.** Discipline makes you take control of your life. It drives the actions necessary to develop good habits, reach your goals, and become the best version of yourself.

4. **Discipline makes you happier.** You achieve happiness by earning it. When you commit to bettering yourself through the disciplined pursuit of your goals, you find happiness along the way.

Developing Discipline

To begin developing discipline, you need to find a reason why you want to improve. Who are the people and what are the goals that drive you? My drive to get up at 5 am came from wanting to change my circumstances and take control of my life.

After ten years of hard work, I qualified as a property lawyer in 2008. My legal career was about to start. Or so I thought. Two weeks before qualifying, I found out that the role I was due to start was being made redundant. The credit crunch had set in and property roles vanished overnight. This experience shifted my mindset. I wanted to control when and how I spent my time working. The only way for me to achieve that was to start my own business.

To develop discipline, you need to identify your motivation for establishing it. You need a reason why you want to make a change. Once you have a reason, you need to decide how you're going to change.

Setting a long-term goal helps—one that's clear, measurable, and challenging. Set a deadline on the goal to inspire a sense of urgency. Keep it in daily focus, so you don't lose sight of what you want to achieve.

I started my cleaning business in August 2012. My goal was to quit work by December 2013 and work full-time in the business. To achieve this goal, I set myself two milestones:

1. Save enough money to cover 12 months of expenses
2. Generate at least £75K revenue.

My morning routine was a constant reminder of the goal I was trying to reach. The first 90 minutes of my day focused on doing the work. I was taking incremental steps towards my goal every day. By breaking my milestones down into daily, weekly, and monthly actions, I had a plan for what I needed to do. This kept me accountable. I knew the next action I needed to take to stay focused and on track. Having a morning routine developed the discipline I needed to achieve my goal. I was building up evidence that I would succeed by putting in consistent effort.

To cultivate and sustain discipline, it's important to establish a reason for it. Once you've identified your drive, decide how you're going to achieve your goal. Break it down into small steps and take action to complete those steps every day. Doing this generates momentum. Momentum builds the discipline required to reach your goal.

Obstacles to Discipline

As you develop discipline, there are days when it fails you. There are overwhelming challenges or obstacles that are out of your control. Letting these influences stop you disrupts progress towards achieving your goal.

Over the last ten years, three recurring obstacles have affected my discipline:

- Procrastination
- The fear of failure
- Factors outside of my control

Procrastination

Procrastination is problematic for several reasons. It causes stress, anxiety, and dread. Procrastination inspires more procrastination in an endless, self-defeating loop. To stop yourself getting caught in this loop, you need to take action.

When I feel myself starting to procrastinate, I use the five-second rule. Created by Mel Robbins, the five-second rule is a simple tool that rewires your mind to positive action. I use it to get out of bed at 5 am, make the next sales call, or have uncomfortable conversations. Here is how it works.

Counting backwards (5-4-3-2-1-ACTION) focuses your brain on the task at hand. In doing this, you distract your brain from its default setting of procrastination. When you count backwards, the five-second rule encourages you to take action. As Mel Robbins explained, "The moment you have an instinct to act on a goal, you must 5-4-3-2-1 and physically move, or your brain will stop you."

By giving yourself zero room to think, you create a virtuous cycle of action. Taking constant action defeats procrastination.

The Fear of Failure

In the early stages of my legal career, I was driven by a fear of failure. The fear of failing to get into law school. The fear of failing to win a training contract. The fear of failing to qualify as a solicitor. Despite having these fears, discipline helped me overcome them. Fearing failure didn't stop me from taking action.

The fear of failing to keep a job after qualifying hadn't crossed my mind. Unfortunately, it was the one thing that came true. The experience stopped me in my tracks. I then started to fear failing to practise as a lawyer, never mind making partner. For almost 12 months I sat with this fear. It stopped me from taking action towards finding a new job. Instead, I spent time looking for opportunities to start a business. I began flipping secondhand designer gear on eBay. I found and sold deadstock hair and beauty products online. These steps gave me the evidence and self-belief I needed to start my own cleaning business.

Rather than using my redundancy as an obstacle to success, it became the catalyst to move in a new direction. I grew even more disciplined to face the challenges ahead.

Factors Outside My Control

After finishing law school, I struggled to win a training contract. Despite sending hundreds of applications to law firms, I rarely made the cut. When I did get invited to an interview, I wasn't the profile they were looking for. So, I changed my approach. I decided to get work experience to use as leverage for future applications.

Over the next four years, I went from being fresh out of law school to managing a team of 12 paralegals at a hyper-growth real estate investment business. That experience landed me a training contract and set me on the path to qualifying as a lawyer.

More recently, I've been practising "fear setting." Developed by Tim Ferriss, fear setting helps you make hard decisions and take action when fear is holding you back. It puts your fears under the microscope. It makes you assess the impact of the worst-case scenario and consider the consequences of taking action (or not).

The Stoics practised *premeditatio malorum*, the premeditation of the evils and troubles that might lie ahead. As the famous Stoic philosopher Seneca stated, "What is quite unlooked for is more crushing in its effect, and unexpectedness adds to the weight of a disaster. This is a reason for ensuring that nothing ever takes us by surprise. We should project our thoughts ahead of us at every turn and have in mind every possible eventuality instead of only the usual course of events."

The Stoics remind us that things don't always work out. By solving challenges and overcoming obstacles in advance, when they do arise, you have a solution at hand. You approach the situation from a calmer perspective and have a clear mind to take action.

That's why I set a target of saving 12 months' expenses. I wanted to give myself the time and space to succeed with my cleaning business. I knew that there would be unforeseen challenges with my start-up. Savings gave me security and peace of mind. It allowed me to focus 100 percent on building my business, instead of worrying about paying rent.

Developing Sales Discipline

Generating at least £75K revenue required me to focus on sales. When I started my cleaning business, I wasn't a natural at sales. It was a skill I had to develop. To hit my milestone, I needed to take a disciplined and deliberate approach to sales. I had to learn new skillsets and develop different attributes. Above all else, I needed to take action. That meant focusing on the most important sales activities every day—prospecting, cold calls and emails, qualifying, and following up.

I developed five sales disciplines to win new clients:

1. The discipline of prospecting
2. The discipline of nurturing
3. The discipline of following up
4. The discipline of improvement
5. The discipline of personal development

The Discipline of Prospecting

I realised that discipline made all the difference when it came to prospecting. By developing this discipline, I gave myself more opportunities at bat. I produced better sales results through disciplined prospecting, regardless of my sales ability. Over the long term, sales results are the product of your prospecting.

Prospecting became my first sales discipline.

The Discipline of Nurturing

Anthony Iannario has stated, "Who you are as a professional salesperson is visible in your client list. If you want to add marquee clients to that list, you have to have the discipline of nurturing." Ninety-five percent of the ideal clients I spoke to already had a cleaning supplier. Through the discipline of nurturing, I focused on providing value up front. I built relationships that ended up creating opportunities.

Opportunities arise when you practise the discipline of nurturing.

The Discipline of Following Up

One practice that I carried over from my legal training was doing high-quality follow-up work. More than sending the email that I promised, I made sure to provide value by going the extra mile. Research, tips, and answering questions all contributed to my follow-up. This made it easier for prospects to say yes to proposals that I sent over.

The discipline of following up shows clients that you can be counted on when they need you to deliver.

The Discipline of Improvement

I learned very quickly that in sales, you can't afford to rest on your laurels. Clients don't care what you did for them yesterday. They want to know what you are doing for them today. That's why I was always looking to improve my service to clients. I shared ideas with clients about how I was planning to create value for them in the future.

Avoid complacency by practising the discipline of improvement. Focus on creating new value to strengthen your relationship with clients.

The Discipline of Personal Development

Because I was new to sales, I spent a lot of time learning. I recognised that for me to succeed, I needed to become the best version of myself. *Me 2.0.* That meant investing time and money to improve the most valuable asset I had—me.

I committed to always learning—reading, studying, and taking notes. The more I invested in myself, the better my sales results became. The discipline of personal development helps you grow, improve performance, and get better results.

By committing to the five sales disciplines every day, I set standards for myself and hit my revenue target. I took 100 percent responsibility for the outcomes that I was producing, good and bad. When things didn't go my way or mistakes happened, discipline helped me detach from the outcome. It stopped the situation from compounding and impacting my momentum.

On days when I thought I needed a break, I took it the next day. Only then did I realise that I didn't need a break, I was lacking discipline. On days when life or my office job got in the way, I got back to practising the sales disciplines as soon as possible. I made sure to never miss twice. Missing one day happened from time to time, but I made sure to never miss two in a row.

The five sales disciplines allowed me to quickly recover from each setback. They helped me to maintain progress towards my goal.

To develop your sales discipline, ask yourself:

- Is prospecting a discipline or something I approach sporadically?
- How do I practise the discipline of nurturing my dream clients?
- Do I keep all of the commitments I make to follow up?
- Do I have a disciplined approach to improving the value I create for clients every month or quarter?
- What are the main components of my personal development plan?

Final Thoughts

Discipline is a skill you can master if you're willing to put the work in. It provides you with the positive constraints necessary to achieve your goals.

Goals are important. They direct action and provide deadlines. Goals can motivate you and provide you with milestones and a way to keep score. When you complete goals, you set new ones.

Discipline is different. It means taking action every day. Discipline is the driver that makes you do the hard things necessary to reach your goals. It's easier to be effective in business when you develop discipline. To achieve the things you want in life, you need discipline.

Discipline is destiny.

About the Author

Matt Harris is an entrepreneur, business coach, and content creator. He sold his cleaning business in 2020 and started The Growth Lab, a growth partner for cleaning and FM businesses. The Growth Lab focuses on strategic partnerships, preferred supplier list and leveraged buyouts as the primary strategies for growth. Along with his team, Matt helps business owners execute these strategies to win more cleaning contracts and 3x top-line revenue.

Matt hosts *The Growth Lab* podcast and publishes *The Growth Lab Substack* for owner-operators in the cleaning industry. His popular YouTube channel includes content on entrepreneurship, productivity, and high performance.

Matt is an Evercoach accredited business and high-performance coach and a certified personal trainer. He earned his bachelor's degree in taxation and law, and is a retired lawyer.

Email: matt@iammattharris.co.uk
Website: https://www.iammattharris.co.uk/peakperformance/
LinkedIn: https://www.linkedin.com/in/iammattharris/
Twitter: @iam_mattharris

CHAPTER EIGHT
YOUR BEST IS NOT GOOD ENOUGH

By Wendy Holtz
Sales Coach and Business Consultant
Austin, Texas

"Would you tell me please, which way I ought to go from here?"
"That depends a good deal on where you want to get to," said the Cat.
"I don't much care where—" said Alice.
"Then it doesn't matter which way you go," said the Cat.
—Lewis Carroll, *Alice in Wonderland*

In all the classes I've taught and persons I've coached, two misclassified, overused phrases that I hear all the time are: 1) "I'm trying" and 2) "I did my best." These have become verbal Xanax for sales teams and are an excuse to settle at mediocre. Where it provides a temporary emotional relief to pressure, it cannot promote an environment of sales excellence in today's atmosphere of business and consumerism.

It seems the current sales environment has shifted to an unhealthy form of interaction, exchange, and "service-level acceptance." Historically, we were rewarded for "trying" and "giving our best" because it was synonymous with stepping out of a comfort zone and taking risks—and maybe even creating something miraculous as a result. Loyalty was rewarded and quality was controlled by a reiterative model that was built from manufacturers, such as

Honda, tested within a Japanese construct that needed to scale quickly. The process was designed for mass consumption, war provisions, and assembly line wage-earners. Surplus was discounted, and color options unnecessary. Loyalty became the result of conforming to "same-ness."

Fast-forward a generation and loyalty is only expressed through membership points and frequent shopper perks. Consumers spend more time conversing with AI than with family at the dinner table. Doing "my best" is demonstrated on a website through a series of double-clicks and page refreshes. As sales leaders, we struggle to equate "my best" to a higher level of acceptance—for us and for them. And so, as a result of a disconnected web of consumer choices, "my best" is no longer good enough.

In my workshops, I get glazed-over looks and searing glares when I approach with my key phrase, "Your best is not good enough." And yet, it is meant to jolt and make even the tenured sales driver rearrange their posture and double-click their attention on something more than my high heels.

True peak performance is never stagnant and never camps on its summit because it never really has one. True peak performance is the evolution of perspective, emotional bravado, and skillset inventory that continues to propel your best to new levels of better. *My best reminds me that there is better. My best is better. My best wants better.*

After a few scribbles on the whiteboard, it is at this moment the biting stares in my audience turn to enamored students—erasing the cheater notes on their wrists, disposing of their chewing gum under their table tops, and pushing the plate of quarter-eaten sugared doughnut to the side. Now, it's time to get to work.

My first drill for them—and for you—is to write down your highest single sale dollar revenue—now scratch it out. (And yes, if you don't have this top number quickly, all the more reason it proves you are settling for assembly line sales practices.) Now, double it, and write that number above your last. This is your new goal. This is your new "best." And here's the secret, I just made this number tangible to you by your saying it, seeing it, and writing it down. In a similar application, this is like shopping for a new car, you "suddenly" see this car on the road and in advertisements all the time. It is not irony, it is tangibility.

Introduction to Stabilizers

"So, what makes this perspective unique, and how should I apply it to myself, my team, and my company?" First, it's not unique unless you use it to create difference. I love a good cabernet sauvignon, but the grape isn't unique, the color isn't unique, the label isn't unique, the bottle isn't unique—what offers me perspective is my palate. And this is what makes the assembly line sales rep so good at being mediocre. You can't know my palate unless you ask me about it! I don't care about your best-seller or your favorite on the menu. I only care about *MY* palate. Thus, "your best" is unique to you and how you choose to make your best, better. And since we aren't sharing wine over dinner, it isn't me who needs to care about your best—*YOU* need to.

Now, the biggest piece of this self-betterment puzzle is to understand your stabilizers. A stabilizer is inherently designed to prevent change and calibrate back to a norm that prevents change, progressive or regressive. In personal development and, by extension, team development, three root stabilizers guard-rail "best" and "better."

Intention, Motivation, and Fear Are Your Stabilizers

Why won't you take the game-winning shot? Why won't you swing at full count? Why won't you offer to present to the board? Why won't you meet your friends and NOT drink this time? Why won't you ask them out first? Why won't you give your son dinner instead of drug money today?

There are two kinds of reinforcers regardless of the stabilizer: positive and negative. When you are having difficulties, the first question to ask is, "What am I reinforcing?" This gives you details about what stabilizers derail your growth, or lack thereof.

Intentionality can be defined as "directed focus to fulfill a mindset path" or as I like to say: a "light bulb moment." Intentionality redirects energy toward progressive principles, regardless of distractions, but it's key to note that those mindsets can be negative, else you are missing the light bulb completely.

Motivation ebbs and flows based on encouragement, incentives, and reinforcers. Motivation is reactive and can easily be identified when the reinforcer runs out. Keep in mind, a motivator can be something that is taken away just as equally as something that is given.

Fear stops a person from increasing. Fear is paralyzing. Fear can only be purged through understanding, exposure, and exerting calm assertiveness to stand against the root of the fear. Fear wins every time until it is challenged and overcome.

Described as a simple poetic relationship:

Intention = Not wasting time, effort, or energy on diversions
Motivation = What the diversion gives you
Fear = The size of the diversion

Application of Intention, Motivation, Fear

To triage where you (and your team) fit within this relationship, assess its rationale. We may temporarily redirect the behavior, but we must address the state of mind causing the behavior in the first place. This is how we trade one vice for another, one addiction for another, one spouse for another. If we don't school the behavior and put boundaries around the intention, chaos is allowed to be the leader. Classify behaviors as reactions—is the response due to an overriding intention, motivator, or fear? The immediate sensation of the experience may feel unpleasant. That's when you know you are at the *Matrix* moment when you decide to take the red pill.

You must be totally clear about your intention. If you don't train (expose) your people, you offer no basis of performance management. If they don't have a strong sales leader, they will do what they think they have to do in order to fulfill their needs (aka stabilizers), rather than the behaviors that lend to "better."

If exposure couples to intention, how do you recognize exposure's message? One way is to recognize that moving forward has no guarantees. The next step requires involvement in a new way. Simply said, what made you an All-American will require more (and more "better") to become a pro-bowler. Thus, what do you see when the motivation flames out? You are left with the afterburner dust of accountability.

Accountability = Movement to ownership and mastery

Relief of fear is a reinforcer too. When fear wins as the stabilizer, you see the will to make it through another day end in an addict's overdose, you see complacency in daily goals such that the sales professional quits needing a calendar, you see the knee replacement turn into the athlete's gambling addiction, and you see resentment in your manager.

Seek to enforce what the "light bulb moment" tells you about redirected energy such that it whispers that "my best [1] my trying." What is my stabilizer I need to acknowledge before my best is better?

Each breakthrough results in greater confidence. It forges sustainable knowledge, wisdom, and influence. In leadership, the first lesson you must learn is the impact of your decisions on yourself before you can grasp the impact of your decisions on others. Your best, therefore, is waiting for you to become better.

I Learned About From ...

I learned about intention from Bumble—that just because you approach your dating pool with authenticity and valor and integrity, doesn't mean they do.

I learned about intention from church—that just because you raise your hands and wear a cross around your neck, doesn't mean you practice faith and talk with God.

I learned about intention from Monopoly—that just because you circle the board to put a hotel on Park Place, doesn't mean your employees smile when they think of you or that your investors haven't maxed out their credit lines.

I learned about motivation when I didn't have any. I learned about motivation from survival school manuals because I had to decide on my own. I learned about motivation from the Tooth Fairy and Easter Bunny—because I wanted to believe in the heart of the thing despite never seeing it. I learned about motivation from cancer—because I didn't have a choice.

I learned about fear from addiction—because it was the one thing that always treated me the same. I learned about fear from not fitting in with the President's Club Circle. I learned about fear from the abuse of my husband. I learned about fear from the school ground laughter such that I never wanted it to be me. I learned about fear from hoping I was enough for them, although it was really me that I needed to convince that I was enough.

With no "keep going" signal (and no reinforcement) the subject develops their own, often resulting in a negative behavior. Principles are intention. Whatever you can tolerate, you cannot change. Principles motivate when motivation doesn't exist, like it's an opposing motivation (i.e., discounting or cutting corners), or as when we are confronted with fear (i.e., giving false truths or never completing the task). Whenever we engage in a habitual behavior in response to something we fear, we reinforce that fear. The best treatment is exposure—eliminate it quickly. Exposure is all about reinforcement in the brain. Overcoming a phobia (threshold) allows you to greatly empower and build confidence that furthers self-esteem.

"Progressively better" becomes exposure, not experience.

Why in Sales

How do you start to apply these things in sales?

- Recognize your assembly line sales mentality—often this takes the form of a "success standard" and how it's defined. Seventy and above is passing, a standard car package, or "at least" as your qualifier.
- Tinker with the pieces off the assembly line—allow yourself to see how you can remove the surplus and create a new color option. Mark my words, your innovation must scale—create lilac as a component of your expanded color palette.
- Categorize your patent—test where it belongs and how it defines against your vision. Outline how you can become more efficient and make it tangible. Get in front of more opportunities faster.
- Build processes guided beyond punching a timecard—create intention for when motivation wanes or is isolated (no team chant, no peer group, no diversity training, no pizza party, etc.). If you don't know what you want, you'll be easily distracted by the limits that motivation can tease you with.

In the animal world, they call it "energy." In the athletic world they call it "grit." In the sales world they call it "the dance." In all of these, it's irrelevant the "why" on that day because your motivation changes, else there wouldn't be a greater-than-50-percent divorce rate. How do you motivate a dolphin? How do you motivate an Olympic record breaker? How do you motivate a President's Club sales achiever?

It seems intuitive to leaders that haven't led high-performing groups, but when you have coached these leaders, you'll find motivation is no longer motivation but discipline. Discipline to my identity, discipline to my process, discipline to my memory. Hence, next-level achievements seek out a new normal, a new disruption, a new routine. My better pushes my best, higher.

The most successful people don't thrive on motivation—they build intentional habits, rituals, and processes that supersede discipline when there is no atmosphere of motivation. And yet motivation can reinforce negative behavior in the absence of balance and boundaries. It is independent of motivation but rather reinforces intentions. It removes the need to make a reactive decision because you already made the decision, regardless of the distractions and diversions.

In that way, I challenge you to consider another equation:

A. If Intention = Proactive,
B. And Motivation = Reactive,
C. Intention ^{1} Motivation; thus, Intention ^{1} Reactive

My principles and intentions don't change quickly, but my motivators and my fear do.

What does intention look like in practice? In sales, it is striving for the sale even though they took away the bonus, or putting in the work even though management is out of the office. In life, it is hosting the Bible study group even though the court case didn't go in your favor or submitting the application again even though you've been rejected 54 times.

Stabilizers offer predictability and consistency, whether you are aware of it or not. They calibrate to an internal mark reflective of values to you and your approach to decision-making.

How many people failed to beat the four-minute mile until Roger Bannister did it in May 1954? And yet, they all had an intention to do so … so why Roger? And how did it happen in cold, wet track conditions (exactly the opposite of expert predictions)? And how was it a year later, three runners broke the barrier in a single race? What changed was a timely growth spurt in human evolution … Not hardly … It was a change in the stabilizer level of the mental model. When it was broken, it became tangible—an exposure not dissimilar to the sugar-doughnuts in the conference room that you weren't craving until I just mentioned it—yet their best in this example could now be better, for them and for us.

Case in point, "counting to three" is an inappropriate disciplinary action for your child. Ultimately, the child learns that they can keep doing what they want with no repercussions and the adult doesn't have to give in to the fear (accountability, that is) to discipline precious Johnny. Because of the adult's fear of accountability, we have reinforced a child's behavior that procrastination is an acceptable model of never having to give up the freedom to be "bad" or "unruly." So as sales leaders, we wonder where the sense of urgency has gone. The secret is that you can't give something you've never had.

In sales, you now have insight on how average or below-average performers make decisions based on fear as a stabilizer that recalibrates to relieving the fear—not willing to make cold calls, quitting after the first objection, not considering creative opportunities, not asking for or giving help, being known for excuses. It's like reinforcing "I don't want anxiety when I'm turned down for the proposal, I don't want to have to be made fun of for being at the top of the leaderboard again, I don't want to answer why my calls aren't ending in appointments, so I just won't make the calls." If your decision-making refers to not having something, you'll never know what you can have because you don't know what you want, albeit you know what you don't want. It's less than a temporal target because there is no true target.

Rationale and Takeaway

If you are reading this, this may be the precise moment to move your or your team's stabilizers—from motivation to intention. And what's the "light bulb moment" that signals that uplevel? Design your model to get over (through) the image you have in your own head. Your best wanted me to remind you that it's excited to see your better!

Don't fill that gap with strenuous "striving" so as to avoid being seen as a failure. Rather, look to the one decision that echoes through to the rest and results in a more targeted level of achievement—to beat the four-minute mile, 4:01.00 was not a success. It wasn't the training method that achieved it, it was the focus beyond the distractions, positive and negative.

Overcoming fear is now directed to increasing exposure, identifying a new approach, and continuing to reinforce that approach over time. Why only out-perform the rivals you can see when you can transform the definition of it? And that's where we as sales leaders and companies must challenge ourselves to challenge our people. *My best reminds me that there is better. My best is better. My best wants better. So does yours.*

About the Author

Wendy Holtz is a sales coach and consultant, speaker, and author who helps individuals and teams build a sustainable strategy and cadence that transcends a check-in-the-box training and three-day improvement blip. Investing over 15 years of experience in multi-faceted approaches and industries, Wendy brings an innovative perspective that delivers actionable strategies and insightful questions with an immediate return. Her athletic and collegiate coaching background provides a unique training and conditioning methodology that develops each sales player uniquely and fosters next-level teamsmanship and management that improves the bench players as well as propels the top performers. Her player-coach mentorship style serves to develop the play call strategy needed when teams must push past the finish line and win in overtime.

Her relationship-based management style has led to numerous contributions with municipal incubators and entrepreneurial strategy, VC pitch strategy, and corporate sales records.

Email: wholtz@igpartnersales.com
Website: https://igpartnersales.com/
LinkedIn: www.linkedin.com/in/wendyholtz/

CHAPTER NINE

NO SALE, NO PROBLEM. NO SALE AND NO LEARNING? BIG PROBLEM.

By Florian Hoppen
Founder, GoToMarket.Ninja, Business Mentor
Düsseldorf, Germany

Be curious, not judgmental.
—Walt Whitman

As kids we loved to learn. We asked dozens if not hundreds of questions every day. "Why?" was top of the list. To succeed in the art of sales we need to tap back into our innate, curious, child-like ability to ask questions. Questions not only satisfy our hunger for knowledge, but *a curious mind is also your key to connection.*

In this chapter, I want to invite you to re-discover and use the strongest sales tool ever created. It is free and all of us humans—including you—have it at our disposal. The name of this powerful sales tool is: curiosity.

To effectively sell, you need to walk in your customer's shoes. This is a delicate balancing act you can only achieve when tapping into the innate superpower of curiosity. So sit back, relax, and get ready to instantly increase your sales output through a few simple actions.

Meet a Friend for Coffee

Our mindset is one of the key levers shaping our behavior. That little something that sports coaches also refer to as "attitude." It is the inner energy or tone that we set with respect to a situation and how we expect the situation to play out. Tapping into our superpower of curiosity when meeting a prospect can be achieved by switching into the right mindset for the moment. So let's go on a short mental journey together, shall we?

Please imagine an old friend of yours. Someone you have not seen for several years—you know… life got in the way. You used to be close, you know them very well, and you care about them. Now imagine that you reach out to this friend and set a coffee date. You anxiously wait for the day to arrive, and when it's finally there, you dress up, leave your house, and walk to the café. Now ask yourself: how would you treat your friend when she finally sits in front of you again? Warm, kind, and with an open heart, right? Would you like to know what is going on in her life? What has happened to her since the last time you met? Do you feel that eager curiosity? Yes? Perfect! This is the exact energy, the mindset, that we want to tap into when we are meeting with a prospect.

You might now say, "Yeah, but I don't know my prospects like I know my friends." That's most likely true. But you want to get to know your prospect, right? After all, you want to establish a connection in order to do business with them, right? Okay. Then let's try to reframe it. It's exactly *because* you don't know this person that you have tons of questions, such as: "Who are you? What is your role? What are your current goals? What is keeping you from achieving said goals?" A question is an invitation to open up, and it is fueled by curiosity. Questions build bridges between souls as they provide your conversation partner with the feeling that you care about them. As Dale Carnegie put it perfectly: "To be interesting, be *interested.*" This mindset will carry you further than any well-practiced pitch deck ever could.

Now before we continue, your brain might still be stuck on the question: "How?" If you don't know what to ask, feel free to tap into the following selection of questions that have worked for me and my clients many times when we wanted to have a positive conversation with a sales prospect:

- *What do we need to talk about in the next 20 minutes, so that you say this was time well spent?*
- *What does a typical day in your life look like?*
- *How long have you been working in your current role?*

- *What do you enjoy most about it?*
- *What do you dislike the most about it?*
- *Which goals are you trying to achieve in the next three to six months?*
- *What is keeping you from achieving these goals?*
- *What are the three typical challenges you are running into during a regular week?*
- *What negative outcomes do these challenges result in?*
- *How do you currently deal with these challenges?*
- *What pains you about these negative outcomes?*
- *If you could ask for any kind of support, help, or solution for a problem, and you could have it tomorrow and it would cost you no money, what would this support, help, solution look like?*

Swing Like a Monkey

With the "let's meet an old friend" mindset and equipped with a set of suitable questions to start, we set ourselves up for winning and to dive into a positively-driven conversation. Let's explore our idea of curiosity being a sales superpower a little further and see how a conversation would unfold after starting with a set of sincere questions.

Do you remember a night with this good friend of yours, where you ended up talking and talking until you realized that three hours had passed without you taking notice? This was a conversation where both of you reached a flow state. When you moved swimmingly from topic to topic, starting at A and ending up at Z, with you catching yourself half-way through thinking: "Wait, how did we get here?" You essentially acted like monkeys moving through the forest by swinging from branch to branch. This conversational flow is playful, easy, natural, messy, fun, and above all energizing. It is the way sales interactions should feel. This form of verbal communication is a manifestation of the very way we are wired—quite literally. It is the way our brain learns and grows, building new connections through impulses it receives. From one point of information to another.

Working in sales is all about making new connections and establishing and nurturing them, while business in a way takes care of itself, as long as we take care of the connection. Bottom line, we are in the business of solving problems in exchange for money. This means that we first need to identify a relevant problem that another person has that is bothering them enough for them to be willing to pay money to get rid of it. The only way to find said problem is through asking a lot of questions, listening attentively, and showing a genuine interest in your conversation partner's everyday life.

Doing so becomes much easier when we channel our inner monkey and swing from topic to topic with our prospects—just naturally. How? Remember the conversations you've had with good friends. The ones where you lost track of time. Remember your level of natural curiosity you applied there, and tap into it. Be authentic, be open, and show vulnerability. Doing so makes it easier for your conversation partner to open up to you. Your goal is to learn as much as possible about them and their everyday life. Why? Because this is how we build trust and rapport with our prospect—which, by the way, is 80 to 90 percent of our work in sales. This information is the foundation upon which we build a suitable offer later in the process.

Dig Like a Truffle Pig

Okay now, we enter a conversation with the right "talking to an old friend" attitude, and we are ready to allow the conversation to unfold naturally and swing from branch to branch like the proverbial monkey. BUT, how does curiosity help us to know which branch to aim for when we jump topics? After all, our goal as a sales professional is to close a deal, right?

That is right and to reach that final goal we need three ingredients: a connection, also known as rapport, with our prospect; a problem—remember we are in the problem-solving business—that our prospect has that is bothering them enough for them to be willing to pay money to get rid of it; and our prospect's trust that we are capable of solving said problem for them. These three items work a little like Russian nesting dolls. You need to establish a connection first, discover the actually relevant problem your prospect is having, and then build your prospect's trust in you that you are the person to get the problem solved.

Let's answer the question of how to pick the right branches to aim for in conversation. First, we want to look out for branches enabling us to build the connection between us and our prospect. A marker we can aim for is our prospect's personal preferences, including their preferred sensory experience, the proverbs and verbal images they use to express themselves, and what they find pleasant or unpleasant.

To figure this out, *you follow the trail of personal interests.* You can connect by mentioning the poster on the wall or a book on the shelf in the background of your Zoom call, or the headset they use, or the fresh tan suggesting the recent return from a holiday, or any other tiny "truffles" you can identify while speaking to your prospect. Like a truffle pig unearthing delicious fungus spores, you may discover that your conversation partner pursues an exciting hobby, has three kids, or has lived and worked for several years in a foreign country.

Once we find a "truffle," something our conservation partner cares about, it's time to dig deeper. We want to ask a genuine question specifically targeted at our customer's point of interest:

- *That's exciting, can you tell me more?*
- *Interesting, how exactly do you understand this?*
- *Who else is involved?*
- *How often do you do that? How did it start?*
- *Why did you choose this country?*

We use these kinds of questions to go deeper into the topic to understand our prospect and through showing our interest, let the connection grow naturally. One word of warning for your search: *show interest and don't pretend!* Humans have a sixth sense for situations that "feel off" and easily see through fake interest—no matter how well you think you can act, your prospect will feel this notion.

Now that we have built our connection, it's time to identify the relevant problem we can solve. To find these we are basically applying the same truffle pig technique again, only this time we use it around topics of our prospect's everyday work life. To transition from the personal to the professional exchange, we can use a transition phrase such as, *"It is so nice to talk to you and sorry that I got carried away with my questions. Shall we invest a couple of minutes to talk business?"* Once our prospect agrees, we can use questions we have already mentioned above:

- *What does a typical day in your life look like?*
- *What does a typical week in your everyday life look like?*
- *How long have you been working in your current role?*
- *What do you enjoy most about it?*
- *What do you dislike the most about it?*

We listen closely to the responses our prospect presents us and dig deeper with follow-up questions like: *"I see, can you tell me more about that? Interesting, how exactly do you understand this? Who else is involved? How often do you do that task?"*

What we are looking to find here are *sources of friction* our prospect is experiencing in their everyday work processes. So after our opening: *"What does a typical week in your everyday life look like?"* We let them describe it and allow them to share details. From said details provided, we look for systemic friction—recurring challenges in their work life resulting from systemic imperfections.

To extract and collect the friction, we ask our prospect: *"Which three things did you stumble upon, cost you time, or annoyed you this past week?"* Whatever the answer may be, for example, "my co-workers," we will be a brave "truffle pig" and dig deeper to find out why the co-workers are a source of experienced friction. Hence, we ask: *"What was the disagreement about? How often does this irritation happen? Every week? Every other week? How do you deal with it today?"*

Following this procedure and allowing our natural curiosity to drive us, we extract the necessary ingredients for a well-placed and impactful sales pitch. As already agreed upon, sales eventually comes down to closing deals. To arrive there, we need to build a connection with our prospects, extract and identify a relevant problem our prospect is struggling with, and build the trust within our prospect that we are the right partner to solve the problem for them.

Building Trust Through Authenticity

Building trust with your customers is crucial to any successful business relationship, and one of the most important factors in establishing trust is authenticity. As a salesperson, it is essential to be your genuine self and not try to project an image of perfection. Your customers will appreciate your efforts to stay honest and transparent, and they will be more likely to trust you if they feel that you are not trying to sugar coat and deceive them. You can double down on your trust-building efforts by working with your prospects and making them your co-pilots uncovering their challenges side by side, instead of presenting them with your perception of their current situation. Avoid sleazy sales tactics to manipulate them, such as collecting yeses or framing. Instead, work collaboratively with your prospect, tapping into both your curiosity batteries and helping them to see the value in what you are offering for their situation.

This will not only build trust, but it will also establish a solid foundation for a long-term business relationship.

Of course, building trust takes time and effort, and it is important to remember that not every customer will be the right fit for your business. However, by being authentic, working collaboratively, and enjoying the conversation with your customers, you will establish a solid foundation of trust that will serve you well in the long run. Beyond that, it is key to remember that every customer interaction is an opportunity to learn and grow. No one has all the answers, and it's okay to make mistakes. As long as you are willing to learn from your experiences and keep growing, you will continue to build trust-based relationships with your customers and establish yourself as a reliable and trustworthy business partner.

Enjoy Yourself

At last, and above all, you want to make sure you enjoy yourself. Just like with good friends, good memories and strong bonds are made through the good times you enjoy with one another. When you ease into a situation and let it flow naturally following the drive of your curiosity, it is almost impossible to have a "bad conversation." Unlike the common belief of "having to act professionally," it's okay to lose track of time and talk to your customers as though you were old friends. If you can establish a friendly rapport with your customers, they will be more likely to trust you and want to do business with you.

So let your conversations flow. Allow yourself to go beyond the scheduled time frames—it is a great sign of growing openness, emotional proximity, and, eventually, trust. Remember that we are human first, so we urge you to double down on allowing your inner child to re-emerge and live out its love for learning and the question, "Why?" Do that and let the "measurable business results" take care of themselves. Yes, we are all in it to achieve sales success, but are we not also on the journey to live a life worth living?

With the right approach, both of these are possible!

About the Author

Florian Hoppen is a seasoned professional with 15-plus years of sales expertise. From intern and apprentice over VP marketing and sales to company founder, Florian has walked his fair share of miles in sales shoes. With GoToMarket.

Ninja (GTMN), he has founded a sales consulting boutique for B2B companies that has mentored and trained 200 -plus start-up teams across 25-plus markets from 2020 to 2023. Combining deep psychological understanding with business strategy acumen, Florian and his team understand the emotional drivers behind every business and tailor sales action plans for maximum impact. Since Florian is driven to help his clients truly connect with their customers to build lasting business networks, GTMN prioritizes customer understanding, simplifies sales processes, and removes guesswork. As a result, they offer actionable guidance, empowering entrepreneurs and sales teams with the skills needed to navigate the dynamic modern B2B sales landscape and successfully deliver their products.

Email: florian.hoppen@gotomarket.ninja
Website: www.GoToMarket.Ninja
LinkedIn: linkedin.com/in/florianhoppen
Instagram: @the_floho

CHAPTER TEN

WILL THE REAL SALESPEOPLE PLEASE STAND UP?

By Loren Kell
Founder, UnorthodoXpressions; Sales Trainer
Guanacaste, Costa Rica

I'm starting with the man in the mirror
I'm asking him to change his ways
And no message could've been any clearer
If you wanna make the world a better place
Take a look at yourself and then make a change.
—Michael Jackson, "Man in the Mirror"

The Two Percent

What does gratitude have anything to do with sales?

This book is about the peak performance mindset, right? And, if you are reading this, you are most likely already ahead of the majority in the sales field. You see, in my humble opinion, the fair majority of salespeople are salespeople for one of a few reasons. Number one, they are undereducated natural hustlers. Meaning they didn't go to or complete college, or high school for that matter, but they needed to make good money and the steps to get to the sale are easily taught and followed. At least enough to make a relatively modest living. That was me in the beginning.

The second reason is because their first, second, or third career choices or college education didn't pan out, and they figured they needed to make good money fast, so they tried their hand at sales. For the most part, this is the salesforce. There is also the two percent. These are salespeople, sales coaches, entrepreneurs, and course creators who do sales because it is in their blood. They have found their sense of purpose and they can't imagine doing anything else. This two percent may also include some of those from the first two categories. Identifying which category (or categories) you fall into is important. Also note: these are only my categories; there may be more. The point to do a self-assessment here—why are YOU a salesperson or aspire to be a salesperson?

Pause for a minute and make that assessment for yourself. Be honest, there is no judgment. It's between you and you anyway.

A More Excellent Way

Will the real salespeople please stand up?

Who are the real salespeople and why are they in sales? The answer is the same reason as everyone else for the most part. The money is great. Well, if everybody is in sales more or less for the same reason, why are there so few top-level salespeople and so many substandard, middle-of-the-road, fill-the-position drones? Most of the time, for most clients or entrepreneurs, salespeople are a necessary evil. Employers are relegated to fill positions rather than choose from the best and the brightest to service their customers and clients.

There is a rare breed of human that is the ideal salesperson, which I believe you are aspiring to become. They are in it, yes, because the money is great and the sky is the limit, but there is an X-factor they bring to the table. Using tools like NLP to (ethically) direct the human mind toward the sale can definitely assist this X-factor, but these too, like the steps of the sale, are external processes. Don't get me wrong! I use NLP and encourage its use. But, it's still only a tool. And that tool is only as effective as the hand of the worker. Do I believe there is a more excellent way or a more excellent companion to the external methods which unlocks our personal X-factors? I do, and it starts with gratitude.

Napoleon Hill, in his bestselling book *Think and Grow Rich,* lays out 13 principles which he gleaned from hundreds of interviews and 20 years of research with the world's wealthiest and most successful people. The first principle is a burning desire. I am not going to give you all the details about what that is according to Hill; you can read the book and thank me later. What I will say is that you CANNOT, in my estimation, have a burning desire apart from gratitude. How so? There is a verse in the Bible that says, "God declared the end from the beginning" (Isaiah 46:10).

Wait, what did God do? Read that again.

Let me explain what that means. Stay with me, this isn't theology, but a truth taught in every culture the world over. Most people read the Bible as though God created everything and everything was. Wrong! God exhibited the burning desire that was harnessed by the settled feeling that the end ALREADY was and—bing-bang-boom—all things came to be. God declared out of the beginning (which technically was before there was anything) what was to be the end and creation lined up to meet that established standard. So, what does that have to do with sales? THIS is the everything part.

If you have seen the movie *The Matrix*, there is a scene where Neo asks Morpheus if he is going to be able to dodge bullets and Morpheus' response was, "When you're ready, you won't have to." When you live from gratitude, you are living out of the closed sale. It is already done BEFORE the customer or client even arrives in front of you. Overcoming objections are like dodging bullets, but like Neo, when you're ready … you won't have to. This is the sales secret that I am going to teach you … but we need to lay some groundwork first.

The Power of Positive Energy

Nikola Tesla said, "If you want to know the secrets of the universe, think in terms of energy, frequency, and vibration." Everything is energy and vibration. When your burning desire is to see your client benefitted, pressed down, shaken together, and overflowing abundantly with the benefits of your particular product or service, you begin to emit a special kind of energy—positive energy.

According to the law of resonance and attraction, you attract what you are, not what you want. Here is the key difference between the supernatural salesperson and the wannabes. If you can learn to live out of the mindset of gratitude, which is the confirmation of the closed sale before you are even with a client, you are sending out positive energy to that client unbeknownst to them. I'm not talking about living out of some false assumption. I'm talking about truly being the salesperson who has the highest client retention and service record of anyone you know.

Confidently living as though it's true, your subconscious mind and the reticular activating system of your brain will begin to confirm it. I am not playing around; this is current-day, empirical neuroscience and yet it's pretty crazy. You have the capacity within your subconscious mind to affect and to direct your sales reality. You can, in fact, learn to intuitively direct to yourself the types of clients you want. You can train your mind to lead you to the sale and to energetically guide your perfect client.

One very important key to making the universe work on your behalf is having at least two beneficiaries when it comes to your desires. I can think of two right off the top of my head—you and your client. The primary beneficiary should be your client, and, as salespeople, we must desire only the highest benefit for our client in all circumstances. Don't worry, you will get paid too, and handsomely at that. This is the secondary beneficiary, trust me.

Okay, assess this for yourself. Are you selling the best product or service available, or are you just selling whatever it is you are selling to make ends meet? You will never get where you want if your client takes a backseat to your personal benefit or desires. And truth be told, living out of the gratitude space will create a dissonance within your inner self when you violate this principle. Just getting paid is the wrong reason to sell anything. It is an amazing benefit, but leveling up your sales is about the service mindset. So let's talk a little about this "mindset" that is going to manifest in your sales peak performance.

The X-Factor

What is mindset development in my view? Babies develop, plants develop, but most of the time in sales, mindset becomes more like land development with strip malls and rigid structures rather than eco developments that use the terrain and natural environment to enhance the expansion. Lanes to follow and slots to park in. A "what to do" and a "where to go." Mindset development often falls into the trap of doing, rather than being. It gets categorized as simply a "check-up from the neck up" or "getting the head in the game." Doing is easy, but it's the being part that takes organic development, like a small human as they grow and become. Mindset development is about personal transformation for the sake of being a better human, a better spouse, parent, or son or daughter LONG before it's about sales. Sales can be so isolating, almost compartmentalized. Customers/clients are relegated to being called simply leads, sent through funnels, and mechanically treated like cattle because the sales system works.

There is no denying the system. The sales system has stood the test of time and weathered the worst of economic storms. The sales method of doing and succeeding is easily replicated and effective at building sales drones that punch the clock, compete for number one, and are commonly found out back smokin', jokin', and havin' a coke. The sales environment when simply left to mechanics and routine tricks and tactics becomes sterile of positive human emotion and loses its sense of purpose.

Way back when, I found myself in auto sales (after a poor showing of door-to-door life insurance). I was good—cocky and arrogant—but good. I knew my stuff; I had all the answers to overcome the objections. Many salespeople don't have any idea what it is like to be on the line, like gladiators trying to grind out a sale, standing in the heat, pounding asphalt, or going door to door. You gotta have grit and you learn a lot about your own personal motivation, but you can get pretty jaded too. It's hard core with long hours, seven days a week, and sometimes going from hero to zero in a month.

Day to day, it was a lot like trying to get laid while eight-minute speed dating (I have never been, but I can imagine). I have a lot of respect for these types of salespeople, maybe I am biased, as that's how I cut my teeth in sales.

Sales and mindset, in their pure form, are fluid processes with ebbs and flows of connectivity with potential or previous clients. Like I, and countless salespeople can attest, the steps to the sale process are a tried-and-true method to get the close. The problem is when salespeople get into the mechanical groove and fail to remember the feeling of what it was like on their first day. The nerves, the energy, the raw human connection, and the open heart and rambling mouth that revealed everything about who that salesperson was, not just about what they were selling. It was totally guileless and transparent. That is what the client is buying. The simple fact is that every customer or client is a buyer, the question is whether or not it will be from you. Did you hear that? You. You are the X-factor. What that means is you better figure out who you really are—mind, body and spirit—if you really want to excel and level up your sales.

Cultivating Gratitude

You are probably wondering, at this point, how to practically get into this gratitude space that cultivates the burning desire and leads to sales. It is easier than you think. It is a process, just like any other. It requires diligent practice and even coaching sometimes. But it can be learned and it should become a life pursuit for you. If your goals in sales are to just close the deal or make the sale, you are living shortsightedly. No, your goal in actuality is to experience the gratitude and satisfaction that can be tangibly felt after you have served your client or customer with the best possible service while making the sale. Gratitude is the goal and gratitude is what you will cultivate while you sleep. Yep, you heard me right, while you sleep. I am going to give you a basic script that you can repeat to yourself as you fall asleep, one for when you wake up, and another for a midday lunch contemplation. Fifteen minutes out of your day to train your conscious and subconscious minds is all you need to start. That's it and the rest will begin to fall into place.

You will still have to know your product and get evangelical, as Ed Mylett in *The Power of One More* would call it, about your cause and really believe in what you are selling. These labors are always going to be required. You are still going to need to set goals, make calls, pound pavement, or whatever your client generation formula requires. And you are still going to be required to be the best human and sales professional you can be. I am not selling you snake oil or some magic pill. Nope, I am giving you the secret edge that even the best salespeople in the world have, but don't necessarily know how to articulate. That's why many of the great salespeople can't teach what they do because they simply don't understand what it is they are doing, they just do it. But you are going to learn the secret to mastering your own mind and mindset, thus creating your own sales reality. Are you ready?

Nuts and Bolts

Keep your hands and feet inside the ride at all times and have fun. Sales should be fun. If you aren't having fun, you really aren't selling, you're a check-stand attendant punching the clock.

Here is a simple three-step process that will only require 15 minutes of your time and a strong book recommendation. Other than the ones I referenced earlier, there is a book called *Sales Power: The Silva Mind Method*. The Silva method is going to teach you very quickly to enter into an alpha state of mind and to readily and efficiently access your subconscious mind, which drives 95 percent of your thoughts, actions, and basically your life. It will also give you some excellent pointers along the way. Get it, read it, study it, practice it, meet your subconscious self, and follow these three steps.

Step One: I am going to give you an example thought to sow into your mind as you enter into your sleep state, but you are going to have to make up your own. WRITE YOURS DOWN! Write it on a three-by-five card, place it in your nightstand, and don't talk about it with anybody. No exceptions. You don't want any outside influence to sow doubt. Got it? Good!

Example: you are having a conversation with your sales manager, coach, team lead, or colleague, and are listening to them tell you how impressed they are with the increase in your close rate. That's it. It is really simple, but it is up to you to write all the details. Can you smell your team lead's cologne or perfume? Do you feel the breeze of the AC in the office? Are you having the conversation over lunch? Are you holding a cup of coffee and what does that feel like in your hand? The more specific you can be, the better. You are going to "experience" these things over and over again until you fall asleep. You want these thoughts to be that last thing on your mind.

Step Two: upon waking up, before thinking or doing anything else, list five to ten things you're grateful for. Quick, like the first things that come to your mind, no matter how deep or surface level they may be. One of them being how your day is going to positively work out and the immensely positive impact you are going to have on your clients, customers, and sales team. Really feel the gratitude and thankfulness. Try to identify "where" in your body you locate and feel it. Practice calling only that feeling up a couple times, don't work at it, but be diligent with practice. Write this list down in a journal you keep next to the bed.

Part Two of Step Two: using the type of detail in step one, imagine/feel a conversation at the end of your day with your sales manager, coach, or team lead congratulating you again on your superior progress and closes. Now go on with your day.

Step Three: midday mindfulness. Find a quiet place. Call your mind back to the early-morning gratitude and end-of-day positive conversation. Envision within your mind that handshake or thank-you email graciously thanking a client for their business. Something really simple to remember and do consistently! Do this purposefully and peacefully for five minutes. Within your imagination, smell the smells, hear the sounds, see the sights, taste the tastes, and feel the feelings. That's it. Go back to work.

Time and practice will show substantial fruit! But here is the deal, DO NOT go digging up the seeds of progress you are sowing into your subconscious mind with doubt and constant progress check-ups. Let your subconscious mind and circumstances fall into place. There is no need to force anything! Gratitude will lend to your hearing your intuitive side leading the sales conversation naturally. Trust yourself, follow your gut, not your head, and pursue the best interest of your client or customer always, and you can never go wrong! Be the authentically infinite YOU and the sales will roll in, no matter what economy you are in. It's up to YOU. You want to have a different outcome? Be different. Don't wait for the conditions to change, look in the mirror, change yourself, and see what happens. I think you will be surprised. Go get it!

About the Author

Loren Kell is a dynamic motivator, visionary, inspirational speaker, and intuitive sales, life, and gratitude coach and blogger. He is colloquially known as the Gratitude Guru. He teaches salespeople how to harness their inner superpower of intuition and authenticity to massively increase sales and skyrocket to new sales heights in addition to helping people discover their soul purpose in sales and in life.

Loren's simple, yet profound, methods help his clients transform their minds, souls, and spirits to incredibly impact their personal and professional worlds, causing them to be not only amazing salespeople, but better husbands, wives, daughters, sons, and human beings.

Located in Costa Rica and living the dream, Loren coaches remotely, meeting his clients right where they are, physically and metaphorically. He strategically offers both one-on-one and group coaching for faster results in addition to active accountability sessions to keep his clients on track.

Email(s): lkgratitudeguru@gmail.com
unorthodoxpressions@gmail.com
Linked in: https://www.linkedin.com/in/lorenkell/

CHAPTER ELEVEN
#GRINDTIME

By Jarvis Leverson
Business & Life Coach for Entrepreneurs
San Diego, California

If you don't work, you won't eat … You don't grind, you won't shine!
—Mike Jones

There's nothing special about me. I had been a pretty average performer all of my life. In fact, I was even fired from several sales jobs before I finally figured it out in my mid-30s. Most of my career was a struggle. I was good at building relationships but horrible at everything else. Managing the sales process, keeping track of opportunities, following up on leads, dealing with issues from current clients, prospecting for new clients, submitting paperwork, managing our internal support teams, producing reports, attending meetings—every day was just a blur and I didn't have a way to keep it all organized. I would get home from a long day and be completely exhausted. The funny thing is that I couldn't even tell you what productive work I got done all day. It's like the day just happened. It's no wonder why I was always at the bottom of the pack, producing mediocre results at best.

This idea of fighting through the day started to create some pretty bad habits in my life. Each night, I would get home and pour myself a vodka soda. After a long hard day, I felt like I deserved it! It was really just my way of numbing myself from the overwhelming stress of the day. This habit of "rewarding myself" after a long hard chaotic day went from just a few nights a week to every single night. It went from just a vodka soda to five drinks back-to-back. It went from just me sitting in front of the TV relaxing to me going out to bars and staying out all night. My work performance went from mediocre … to dismal … to not even showing up at all. It got to the point where my performance was so low, my name didn't even show up on the scoreboard in the office.

After getting let go from my third sales position in five years, I had to move back in with my mother to restart my life. I moved out of my mother's house at 22 right after graduating from college and went off on my own as an official adult. So, you can imagine that moving back in as a 35-year-old man was devastating to my pride. It was at that moment, feeling completely deflated and defeated, that I had to put the pieces of my life back together again.

So, there I was, laid up on my mother's couch, watching YouTube videos one day when I came across a video by Jim Rohn. In the video, Jim Rohn said something that has stuck with me till this day: "Every result that you are getting in your life is your fault. If you want a different result, you have to do something different."

This was a punch to the gut! I was good at blaming everything else for my failures: "It's the economy," "It's the changing market," "They gave me a bad territory," "The other reps got all the good clients," "My manager just doesn't like me." In one sentence, Jim Rohn put the blame squarely on my shoulders. It was my fault. The results that I was producing were a direct reflection of the things that I was doing. If I wanted different, then I had to be willing to do different. At that moment, sitting right there on my mother's couch, I finally took ownership of my life.

I started reading books to figure out the "formula for success." I wanted to know what it was that allowed some people to achieve extraordinary results while others just lingered in an average, mediocre zone of life, not ever living up to their full potential. Do the achievers have special powers? Are they born that way? Is it some secret sauce that others don't know about?

I started studying the habits and routines of some of the most extraordinary achievers on earth like Warren Buffet, Kobe Bryant, Bill Gates, Michael Jordan, Tony Robbins, and Oprah Winfrey. I started dissecting their mindsets, beliefs, and behaviors so that I could reverse-engineer their "winning formulas" and apply them to my life.

As I read about each person, I started noticing a pattern. Kobe would wake up early and go to the gym and shoot 200 free throws before practice would start. Warren would wake up early and read financial reports before he started work. Tony would wake up early and meditate and exercise before he met with his team. Each person had a practice of waking up early and working on themselves and their dream before they started their workday. And by doing so, they controlled the day, instead of the day controlling them.

This was eye-opening for me. Prior to this realization, I never had any intention to my mornings. I would just wake up and go. I had this "just in time" mentality. I squeezed out every minute of the snooze button before waking up "just in time" for the first thing that I had to do for the day. I would wake up "just in time" to race to work or "just in time" for my first appointment or "just in time" to deal with family. I never had any buffer space in my mornings to get planned, prioritized, and organized, and to set the tone for the day. Therefore, I never felt like I had control of the day. Before the time my eyes opened, I had been in a constant state of reacting and responding to the day. Every email, every notification, every text message, every fire that needed to be put out, every interruption, every distraction, every request, every family matter—I serviced everyone else's intentions because I never took time to establish my own.

That day, I decided to start waking up at 5 am to do a structured morning routine before I started the day. That first hour was just for me—no phone, no TV, no family. It was time for me to journal my goals, get clear on my vision, do some meditating, set my intentions for what I needed to do for the day to be a success, plan out my day, and then do some exercise. I called this my #GrindTime.

Within 30 days of me initiating at least 60 minutes of undistracted alone time every morning (#grindtime), I got my real estate license. Within 60 days I signed with a broker in San Diego and officially moved out of my mother's house. Within 90 days, I was the fastest-growing real estate agent in the office.

It's crazy how quickly my life turned around with this simple concept—waking up a little earlier with a structured routine to set my intentions for success before I started the day. Every morning, I would wake up with such power, vigor, and momentum that it felt like I was a superhero. Every morning, I turned into a hero, and that's how the morning hero was born.

In my real estate brokerage, I was always the first person in the building. By 7 am, while most agents were just having their first cup of coffee, I was already firing on all cylinders. I had already created my prospecting list for the day, followed up with all the deals in my pipeline, created a marketing email, and organized my meetings for the day. One day, the head broker walked into the office and saw me sitting there #grinding away in the dark and said, "Dude, it's like you're a superhero first thing in the morning!" From there, he started calling me the morning hero.

The following week, he asked me to speak at our weekly team training to show the team what I was doing to be so effective. That was the first time I presented my #GrindTime morning routine to other people. There were five agents in that workshop. By the end of the year, three of those five agents had their names placed on the wall of fame in our office where they were recognized for their outstanding sales achievements.

#GrindTime doesn't just work for me. It can work for everyone. And now I'm going to break down how it can work for you. It's so simple, you might initially underestimate how powerful it is. But this is the same formula that took me from homeless and helpless to sales superhero in just three months. This is the same process that put three out of five sales agents on the wall of fame in their first year. And this simple blueprint can ignite your superpower—not just in sales, but in anything that you want to achieve in life. It's broken into three steps—RISE, GRInD, and SHINE.

Step 1: RISE

As I studied the most epic achievers of our time, I noticed that they all woke up really early. Why is that? Why is there a correlation between early risers and success? Simple. It's called the "whirlwind."

The whirlwind is the chaos of life. It's everything that demands your attention from the moment your eyes open to the moment they close at night. Family obligations, client issues, breaking news, the kids, the dog, the car needs to be fixed, what your spouse needs you to do, distractions, interruptions, text messages, phone calls, emails, chores, errands—you name it.

The problem that most people have is that they wake up right into their whirlwind. By the time they wake up, the world is already active. Messages are flying in. Notifications are dinging. Their kids are awake and need to be tended to. As soon as their feet hit the floor, they get swept away by their whirlwind and their whole day is just a vicious swirl of chaos. They spend the entire day being busy, but they don't do anything really productive. They were just in reactive mode all day.

Outrageously successful people have figured out that if you want to defeat your whirlwind, you have to get a head start over it.

For me, that meant waking up at 5 a.m. There's just a peace and serenity in the darkness of the morning. I call it—my sanctuary. There are no phone calls, no text messages, no breaking news, no interruptions or distractions. The birds aren't even chirping yet. It's a quiet stillness that can't be matched by any other part of the day. There's something magical that happens in that stillness. I call it—strokes of genius. It's where the universe speaks to you. You get new ideas, fresh perspectives. You solve problems and have aha moments. It's like you start receiving all the answers to all of your questions. I believe that the universe is always trying to speak to us, but we can't hear it above the noise of the day. In the morning, it's quiet enough for us to hear the whispers of the universe.

The other big benefit of the morning is that your brain is at its highest cognitive functioning about 30 minutes after you wake up. This means you think more clearly and process things faster. When you combine the fact that your brain is operating more powerfully with the fact that you have undistracted time to focus, you can get twice as much done as normal hours. This is how you bend time. For every one hour of undistracted alone time you have in the morning, you actually get two to three hours of productivity.

I currently wake up at 4 a.m. That's because I have two kids who wake up around 6 a.m. That gives me a solid two hours of #grindtime before they wake up. When you factor in the time-bending effect of those #grindtime hours, I'm actually getting about six hours of productive work done before my day even gets started. This is how I'm able to be done with my entire workday by lunchtime so that I can do something fun with the kids every afternoon—#donebylunch.

An early start means an early finish, so you can have better results while living a more extraordinary life.

Step 2: GRInD

Now that you're getting up early, it's time to #GRInD! The GRInD is your morning routine. It will set the tone for the day. Just like a row of dominos, if you knock down the first domino, it will knock down all the other dominos with ease. Your morning routine is your first domino. Knock it down right, and the rest of the day is easy. The word "GRInD" is actually an acronym for the routine. Let me explain how it works.

G is for goals. Start each day in front of a journal and write your goals. This is to set your focus for the day. It also ignites the law of attraction, which states that you attract what you focus on. When you write your goals every morning, you are bringing them to the forefront of your mind, so all day long you will focus on doing things that align with those goals. You will attract people and opportunities that align with those goals. I say that the universe rewards those who are very clear on what they want and who write it down every day. Writing your goals is your way of telling the universe what you want. And you'll notice how things will just start lining up in your favor.

R is for reflection. In your journal, answer these two powerful questions: "What did I do well yesterday?" and "What could I have done better?" This will help you reinforce the good behaviors that will lead to your success and highlight the areas that you can improve upon. This will ensure that every single day you are better than you were the day before.

IN is for intentions. Based on the goals that you wrote down, now it's time to set your intentions for the day. What are the most important things that you have to get done? Brainstorm all the things that will make this a successful day. This is basically your to-do list, but it's more powerful than just a to-do list because it's based on your goals. It's not just random things like "feed the dog" or "go grocery shopping." Since you wrote your goals first, this is a more focused list of actions intended for you to make progress on your goals. Once you have the list, put a little star next to your top three to five actions. You have just defined what a winning day looks like.

D is for design your perfect day. Once you have set your intentions for what a winning day looks like, it's time to schedule it out on your calendar. If it's not on your calendar, it won't get done. Your calendar is where your commitments are. If you just have a list of things you want to get done, you are just hoping that at some point in the day, you get those things done. But when you actually block out time on your calendar to do them, you fully commit to them, and studies supporting this, showing that you are 90 percent more likely to do them. Go hour by hour in your calendar and schedule your intentions for that hour.

When you design your day, you'll notice that your day will feel much more controlled and smooth. You won't have to think about what to do. You just look at your calendar and execute. I call this, stress-free productivity.

This routine only takes about 15 to 20 minutes to do. Just wake up early (RISE), grab your coffee, sit in front of your journal, and #GRInD! You'll be more focused, you'll be more in control of your time, and you'll be ten times more productive each day. All because you took time in the morning to set your intentions before the whirlwind had a chance to carry you away into a sea of busy-ness.

Step 3: SHINE

Consistency is the name of the game. Let's do a quick thought exercise. If I gave you a penny and asked you to double that penny every day for 30 straight days, how much would you have on the 30th day? No fancy math. No tricks. Just do one simple thing. Double the penny every single day for 30 straight days. How much would you have on the 30th day? A thousand dollars? Ten thousand dollars? You would actually have $5,368,709. Can you believe that? You would have over five million dollars from doing something as simple as doubling a penny every day consistently for 30 straight days.

Now let's take it a step further. What if I said, just double the penny every other day for 30 days. Just slack off on your consistency a little bit. Every other day is still pretty good, right? How much do you think you'll have? Most people would think 2.5 million dollars. That's a logical guess. Five million dollars for full consistency, so 2.5 million dollars for half consistency. Actually, the answer is $327. Can you believe that? Five million dollars for every-day consistency and $327 for every other day consistency.

That's the big difference between average people and extraordinary people. Average people stick to their discipline every now and then. They wake up early every now and then. They journal their goals every now and then. They set their intentions for the day every now and then. If you want outrageous success, you have to RISE and GRInD ... Every. Damn. Day!

Take the 30-day challenge! Try this process for 30 straight days and see how it impacts your life. Commit to waking up at least one hour earlier for undistracted alone time. Commit to writing your goals, reflecting on your progress, setting your intentions, and designing your perfect day in your journal. Commit to sticking with it for 30 straight days. If you make that commitment, I guarantee that 30 days from now, your life will be unrecognizable. Go to http://tribe.themorninghero.com to join the 30-day morning hero challenge.

About the Author

Jarvis Leverson is a highly sought-out speaker, trainer, and coach for entrepreneurs. His "winning formula" has been taught to companies, teams, organizations, and individuals helping them ten-fold their focus, time management, and productivity.

Jarvis is the creator of the Morning Hero Journal also known as the Zero Calendar, which is a five-step journaling routine that entrepreneurs use to plan, organize, and prioritize their day, eliminating procrastination. It has proven to help entrepreneurs gain up to four hours of wasted time each day.

Jarvis is also founder of the Accelerated Growth Club, which offers life-transformative events designed to help people become the best versions of themselves. To date, over 2,500 entrepreneurs and business owners have attended his events helping them live a life of purpose … on purpose!

Email: jarvis@themorninghero.com
Website: www.themorninghero.com
Social Media: @The.MorningHero (Instagram)

CHAPTER TWELVE
SELF-CONFIDENCE IN SALES

By Adrian Logan
Sales Coach & Trainer, Military War Veteran
Bath, England, United Kingdom

*Our doubts are traitors and make us lose the good
we oft might win, by fearing to attempt.*
—William Shakespeare

I first read the above Shakespeare quote whilst studying the play *Measure for Measure* for my A level English exam. I was 16 at the time and racked with all the doubts teenagers have.

When I went into sales and then sales professional development, these words stuck with me. As a wise old sales manager told me, "You will lose every sale you don't go for."

More often than not, what holds us back is self-doubt or the lack of self-confidence. Indeed, I now spend a lot of my coaching of salespeople looking at and developing their self-confidence.

When I talk to friends and colleagues about this, a typical reaction is, "Why do you need to develop the self-confidence of salespeople? Aren't all salespeople confident, isn't it a requirement of their job?" I'm asked this on a regular basis as it's generally perceived, certainly in my country the United Kingdom, that salespeople are all oozing with confidence, even to the point at times that they are considered arrogant or aloof. However, my experiences working with salespeople for over 30 years would suggest otherwise.

Very often when I'm coaching salespeople on a one-to-one basis, I ask them to complete one or more psychometric tests before we start, as I find the results can save time and help us both get to the core of the matter very quickly. I would confidently state that, based on my experience, salespeople are no more and no less confident than the average, and not the super-confident person public perception would have us believe.

Let me give an example.

In 2021, I had a sales team of nine very experienced sellers and their sales manager complete a psychometric test on mental toughness. One of the four traits was confidence, with two elements involved, confidence in their own abilities and confidence in interpersonal interactions. The scale was one to ten (one being low).

The salesperson who had won salesperson of the year twice in recent years scored six (marginally over average) on confidence overall, with the two elements scoring six (abilities) and five (interpersonal). During our one-to-one discussion, this person told me that they were constantly racked with doubt, so they prepared, prepared, and prepared for meetings to compensate.

Is There Any Research About Self-Confidence to Support My Experience?

Not specifically about salespeople, but in March 2023, a report called "The Most Surprising Self-Confidence Statistics and Trends in 2023" was published on Gitnux. Some of the findings:

- 93 percent of people believe that self-confidence is critical to professional success.
- 85 percent of people report struggling with self-confidence issues at some point in their lives.
- People with low self-confidence earn on average $8,000 less per year than people with high self-confidence.
- 70 percent of people attribute part of their career success to self-confidence.

So, confidence is not only important, it can be rare, it's most certainly valuable, and it is career-enhancing!

In a *Psychology Today* magazine piece, the definition of confidence is, "a belief in oneself, the conviction that one has the ability to meet life's challenges and to succeed—and the willingness to act accordingly. Being confident requires a realistic sense of one's capabilities and feeling secure in that knowledge." Furthermore, "Projecting confidence helps people gain credibility, make a strong first impression, deal with pressure, and tackle personal and professional challenges. It's also an attractive trait, as confidence helps put others at ease."

So let's look at that definition and ask—why is confidence especially important for salespeople?

Look back at the definition:

- *To meet life's challenges and succeed*
- *Gain credibility*
- *Tackle challenges*
- *Put others at ease*

If these are not key attributes for a salesperson, I'm not sure what are!

What Aspects of Their Role Do Salespeople Lack Confidence In?

The answer is the salesperson's ability to ask questions, answer tough questions, cold call ... and these are many of the individual activities that salespeople have to perform to succeed.

This often leads to a discussion about introverts or extroverts being better at selling, as many of those tasks would suit extroverts many people believe.

Well, let's put aside the usual image of an extrovert (first on the karaoke machine) and introverts (wall flowers who are shy and retiring) and think of them in this light:

Introverts are energised from within; they are "battery-powered."

Extroverts are energised from external stimuli; they are "solar-powered."

Consequently, we now have a category called ambiverts, who are at times comfortable either on the karaoke or within their own company. The key point here is that introverts, extroverts, and ambiverts can all have low self-confidence.

Another area where salespeople (and others) often lack confidence is in themselves as people. In the UK, salespeople are generally not held in as high regard in society as they are in other countries. This can exacerbate an already fragile view of themselves resulting from their background. In my coaching sessions, I spend the first hour learning about the individual, their background, their upbringing, their school experiences. I'm amazed at the relationships or events they confide in me that have resulted in them having low self-confidence.

Their physical attributes—hair (colour or lack of), teeth, and weight—can also chip away especially in an era of self-image.

What Do Typically Unconfident Salespeople Do?

This surprising lack of self-confidence can result in numerous (counter-productive) behaviours. Below are some:

They present their services to everyone and anyone who will listen (but not for long). This typically happens because the salesperson has been filled with product knowledge, they have memorised it and are just waiting to show how much they know, so talking about it is in their comfort zone. The prospect then mentions something to do with the product, which triggers the salesperson to go on a long ramble about their products, and even open up a PowerPoint presentation. This is guaranteed to induce severe boredom in buyers, but from the seller's perspective, they are back in their comfort zone.

The salesperson then feels downhearted when rejected. This is only natural as most of us like to be liked, and a rejection for a salesperson means no revenue from that prospect. I have seen this result in many different forms of reaction, from despair to anger, none of which will help the situation or contribute to the salesperson's confidence.

The next action from salespeople is chasing prospects to "just check in" or "touch base." If they were skilled and confident, they would have asked the prospect during the discussion about the decision-making unit (people) and the decision-making process, especially timings and when it would be appropriate to "check in." The salesperson thereby handicaps themselves even further by then having to decide themselves when is a good time. The buyer can then view them as desperate (follows up too quickly) or disinterested (follows up too slowly). It's a vicious predicament that their lack of self-confidence has got them into and is making it worse.

Basically, the salesperson's lack of confidence transmits to their prospects, who then harbour doubts about buying from the salesperson ... which erodes the salesperson's self-confidence even more.

So what can be done about it? Here I'll outline some recommended techniques.

Recommended Techniques to Overcome a Lack of Self-Confidence

This is my favourite. I do it myself if I feel I'm slipping.

I call it "three-a-day," and it doesn't involve eating fruit or vegetables!

Here's the logic. Our brain looks forward to tasks yet to be completed. Sometimes that is today, this week, next month, or even further ahead. For example, I'm working on a holiday I plan to take ten months from now.

The brain rarely looks back, certainly not as often as it looks forward. The result is a frame of mind that entails "what we have yet to achieve" as opposed to "what we have achieved."

Allow me to suggest an analogy: imagine you are walking up a steep hill. It's hard work; you're tiring and may be even harbouring doubts about your ability to get to the top. This isn't helped by looking up to see how far is left to go.

- Stop.
- Look down.
- See how far you have come.
- Put your progress into the context of how far is left to go.
- Then walk on with renewed determination and confidence.

I hope you see this as a metaphor for achieving your sales target.
Here's what you can do:

1. Get a small notebook, or if you prefer not to use paper, a separate Note on your mobile phone or Word document on your laptop.
2. At the end of each day, write down three things you are proud of or glad to have achieved. They may not all be major achievements, but that's okay, just capture three. (I recommend pen and paper as physically writing words is meant to help them stick in your memory better.)

3. Do this every day for a week. At the end of the week, look at the 15 things you have achieved this week. I will wager a reasonable sum that you will have forgotten around half of them! This should enable you to end the working week with increased confidence.

4. At the start of the next week, when you have lots of tasks to achieve, then re-read the 15 from the previous week. This should start your week off with increased confidence (and momentum).

5. Continue capturing your three-a-day and at the end of week two, look back on the 30 things you have achieved in the previous two weeks. I wonder how many from the first week you will have remembered. This should act as a strong reminder of what you have achieved and should feel confident about.

6. And so on. At the end of the month, reward yourself and your loved ones with a celebratory event (a meal, a drink, a walk, a movie, whatever).

7. If you do it every working day, over a year, working 200 days you would record 600 achievements! Skim through the 600 achievements on the first working day of the new business year when you are facing your new target and your sales are zero.

8. Use this as your confidence-building motivational action guide.

Rehearsing

Focus the three things on the areas you wish to develop, e.g., interacting with others, cold calling, presenting to your boss.

Rehearse (sometimes called role play) these things. Sports teams, the military, actors, and world-class presenters all rehearse, rehearse, rehearse. And get feedback. Then rehearse again. And again. Until it is "second nature." If people in other engaging activities spend a lot of energy rehearsing, why shouldn't you?

My experiences on the value of rehearsal are as follows.

In the military, if you are a member of a combat unit, you are either preparing for deployment or you are deployed. In other words, you're either practising or doing. The more you practise, the easier the doing becomes.

In a personal or business context, I often present to various-sized audiences. The last high profile one I did about my experiences in the Falklands War. After the presentation, a number of people complimented me on how easy and natural my delivery style appeared. They were quite surprised when I told them I had rehearsed it more than 20 times before I delivered it.

Practise, rehearsal, role play, call it what you will, but the impact on your self-confidence is immense.

Positive Self-Talk

CBT (cognitive behavioural therapy) suggests that our thoughts affect our feelings, which affect our behaviour, and we thereafter behave in a way in order to prove ourselves right ("I can't cold call").

Aligned to this is the concept of a growth mindset. This was first introduced by Carol Dweck and seeks to assess an individual's propensity to practise and learn by placing them on a continuum from a "fixed" to a "growth" mindset.

So, for example, someone who says, "I can't," displays a fixed mindset whereas the one who says, "I'll try to learn," displays a growth mindset. Whilst the concept has been subject to a degree of criticism from the academic community, it has caught the imagination of people involved in people development as a way of encouraging learners to open their minds and grow by trying (and learning) new things.

If a seller would replace "I can't cold call" in their self-talk with "I'm going to strive to get better at cold calling," they would be displaying a growth mindset.

Its value in developing self-confidence is it gives us all the words to say to ourselves for positive self-reinforcement.

Other Common Confidence-Building Techniques

Set achievable goals. Break your large goals into smaller ones. Accomplishing small tasks can help boost your confidence and motivate you to continue setting and reaching goals.

Learn from mistakes. Instead of dwelling on your failures, try to learn from them and use them as an opportunity to grow and improve. Back in 1900 Theodore Roosevelt is attributed with saying, "The only man who never makes a mistake is the man who never does anything." A growth mindset will help here: "I made a mistake, but this is what I learned and this is what I'm going to do differently next time."

Surround yourself with supportive people. Being around people who believe in you and support your goals can help boost your self-confidence. Jordan Peterson's third rule from his bestselling book *12 Rules for Life* is: "Make friends with people who want the best for you." Why surround yourself with people who chip away at your self-confidence? Remember what I said about my coaching sessions earlier.

Take on challenges. Stepping outside of your comfort zone and trying new things can help you build confidence in your abilities. Cast your mind back to when you first attempted something that, at the time, you felt was difficult but now you do it without thinking, for example, driving a car.

And finally, when people compliment you on something you do well, accept the compliment. Positive feedback from others can reinforce the positive self-talk and the "three-a-day" you have been practising solitarily. The obverse of this is to give compliments to others when they deserve it. Their self-confidence may not be as robust as it seems and so they will appreciate your kindness and may even compliment you in return. Good manners cost nothing.

To Summarise

- Confidence is vital in sales.
- We are rarely as confident as we'd like to be in many situations.
- Self-confidence can be developed, especially by using the "three-a-day" technique in a disciplined manner.
- Surround yourself with people who support you. Try to avoid those who drain your confidence.
- Accept compliments. Give them too!

About the Author

Adrian Logan has been working with salespeople for over 30 years, helping them to become better. He is a certified coach, having passed the qualifications for the European Mentoring and Coaching Council. He currently spends his working time coaching a wide range of salespeople and managing development projects for clients.

Prior to moving into sales, Adrian served eight years in the British Military, ending up as a Captain in the Parachute Regiment, with whom he saw active service in the 1982 Falklands War.

Adrian lives in Bath, England, with his wife and two dogs. His two children are now grown up. In his spare time, he supports and raises money for veterans, is a novice fly fisherman, and is interested in most sports.

Email: adrian@adrianlogan.co.uk
LinkedIn: https://www.linkedin.com/in/adrian-logan-2354538/

CHAPTER THIRTEEN

GENERATING IDEAL CLIENTS WITH A SERVING MINDSET

By Bryan McDonald
Sales and Revenue Coach
Chicago, Illinois

Selling is serving, helping others find solutions, impacting lives positively with passion and integrity.
—Farshad Asl

People often ask me, "Does having a serving mindset really work?"

I can definitively say yes. However, there are a few conditions—you have to generally want to help other people, have a desire to make a significant meaningful impact in their business, and lastly, enjoy connecting with other people. If you can say with integrity that you're about all of those things, then this will work. If you don't care about that stuff, I guarantee this won't work.

Shifting into a mindset of serving rather than selling can be a significant advantage and asset in consultative sales. When experts, consultants, and alike adopt a serving mindset, they prioritize understanding their customers' needs, challenges, and goals. Rather than focusing solely on closing deals, they seek to build relationships based on trust, empathy, and genuine care.

Think about the last time you interacted with a sales person where they spent more time telling you what you want instead of allowing you to tell them what you want. Frustrating, right? You see, we all have a deep desire to be heard and understood, and we live in a world where people just try to scream louder or scream more to be heard and understood. When you take a serving approach to consultative sales and allow someone to be genuinely heard and understood, you stick out. The experience you give someone is differentiated, and they make an assessment that their life is better off with you in it than without you.

This approach gives you the ability to listen and understand, so you can tailor your solutions to address specific pain points and offer the most relevant products or services. Consultative sales is quickly turning into a relevance game more than anything now. So, you have to co-create offers with prospects that are target at their specific pain points to create relevance with them. There is a lot of competition in the marketplace, so you have to stick out in as many ways as you can.

Instead of pushing products or services onto customers, you act as trusted advisor, offering guidance and expertise to help clients make informed decisions. This approach fosters long-term partnerships and customer loyalty, as clients feel valued and supported throughout their journeys.

This level of attentiveness and customization creates a distinct competitive advantage, as customers appreciate the individualized attention and are more likely to choose a provider that genuinely understands their needs.

So, the questions are—how do you get into this mindset and how do you operate this way? I'll explain (1) how you experience it, (2) how the buyer experiences it, and then talk about (3) how to get it done. This way you know the orientation and how to approach it, so you can start doing it for yourself today.

1—How You Experience It

It Takes the Pressure off You

Many people I have met, have so much sales hesitancy it keeps them from the success they deserve. They need to bring on clients but hate the things needed to accomplish it. It's like torture, but sales doesn't have to be that way. It can be enjoyable for anyone.

A serving approach to sales feels more natural because the orientation of serving others is a natural state for all of us. We're built to do that. Exploring how to help someone versus selling to them just makes you look at the situation differently. Getting a "sale" is way more stressful than figuring out how to help someone. It's a mindset that just feels different. There isn't a tug of war between you and the buyer, as you are both working toward the same goal.

You Learn How to Get Out of Your Own Way

Selling through serving gets exciting and exhilarating for a lot of people because you start learning what's possible for yourself. We all can be our own worst enemy, and the stories we tell ourselves around selling somebody a product or service has a lot of negative undertones. Things like: "They are going to judge you," "They're going to think you don't really want to help them and just want to sell them something," or "You're just trying to take advantage of them, so you can make money." These stories get in the way of mindsets that produce results for you.

Serving is a mindset that allows you to have stories that are productive, positive, open to possibility, and that allow you to operate from a space of feeling authentic. One of the biggest challenges people in sales situations have is that they have negative stories that generate anxiousness, nervousness, and uncertainty. These all get reduced greatly or removed in a serving approach to sales.

You Become Fully Present with Someone and Not All Inside Your Head

The service approach allows you to feel like you are more in control of your actions and the situation because you're calm, collected, and present. Salespeople feel like they "fail" when sales meetings and prospect situations get out of control. When you are not operating from a space of fear and anxiety, you don't miss things you should have seen or heard, you ask questions or make statements that are very appropriate and on-point, and you maneuver through situations with ease and confidence.

Most importantly, you also start learning how you can make a meaningful impact with the business or business owner. Many of my clients have told me that this gives them more purpose and fulfillment in their craft and chosen expertise.

2—How the Buyer Experiences It

You Fulfill a Basic Human Need

First off, this approach gives the buyer an experience that they have been longing for but are convinced doesn't exist. You fulfill the buyer's need to feel heard and understood. It's something that is engrained in all of us—we want other people to "get us" because that is deeply lacking in the world we live in because we are so divided and separated.

Maslow's hierarchy of needs describes that we all have a desire for "belonging." We want to feel that we are a part of something. So, giving buyers the opportunity to be heard and understood creates a sense of community—aka, a sense of belonging. Buyers want to feel that they can address their issues and concerns with you as part of a team. When you are part of the team doing this, buyers don't feel like you are an adversary "selling" them something. They feel that you are both "sitting on the same side of the table," working together. They then make an assessment that their life is better off with you in it than without you.

They Don't Feel Like They Are Being Sold Something

No one wants to be sold, but everyone wants to buy. By default, buyers immediately assess that you are going to "sell" them. With the serving mindset they quickly realize you're not trying to sell them something. It becomes, in neuro-linguistic programming terms, a pattern interrupt. They expect your behavior to be a certain pattern and when that pattern doesn't show up, they can't respond like they usually do. This in and of itself allows them to view you differently. What it practically does is it creates a safe space for them to be transparent and truthful. All of which is helpful to you and them in the sales process. Traditional sales tactics make buyers closed off and only tell you half-truths because they feel it's a "me versus you" orientation because they are being sold something and not getting help.

They Realize That Your Agenda Is Actually Their Agenda

Control is a dynamic that is being jockeyed for in sales conversations. Buyers and sellers both want it. Buyers are constantly trying to stay on their agenda as a tactic to not be sold something that isn't a fit or a need of theirs. Consciously and subconsciously, they are worried that if they get off their agenda, they will lose control and waste time in a meeting with you. So, following their agenda allows them to open up and reveal more. They realize they don't have to play the games that they usually play in defense of trying to stay on their agenda.

3—How to Get into the Mindset and Do It

Detach from the outcome. First and foremost, I'm not saying, don't care about the outcome or don't prep for the outcome. What I am saying is, don't hold on to the outcome that you want so deeply that it gets in your way. The biggest challenge people have is wanting the outcome to happen so much that they can't be present in the moment. To serve someone you have to be fully present and paying attention, as well as listening to figure out how you can serve them, and if you can at all, at that.

Get really clear on your ideal client. For this you have to know who it is and who it isn't that you serve. Full clarity is knowing both sides of the coin. Because when you don't know both sides, what happens is we try to take someone that kind of looks like an ideal client, and then we convince ourselves that they are. When you know who your ideal client is, you know how to listen for the problems that they have, in the specific ways that they have them. This way you really are clear about what's really going on with them. Buyers want you to really understand not only what problems they have but how those problems affect them. This gives you so much insight into their world that it allows them to assess that you are there to help and not just to sell.

"No" has to be an option. What I mean by this is that you both—seller and buyer—have to have "no" as a valid option in regards to working together. You must be able to walk into meetings, knowing that you can and may decline moving to the next step with as much power as the buyer has to do that. Without that you can't be fully present and listen to someone when all you're trying to do is get that person to say yes.

The paradox that this creates is the fact that the more meetings you enter with "no" as an option, the more sales meetings you are going to have. Prospects, clients, and referral resources will introduce you to other prospects because they know that you are someone that's a low-risk introduction. They understand that you are just going to come in and understand their situation and not move forward unless it's a good fit. People will be more than happy to introduce you and say things like, "No matter what, Bryan will just help you figure out what the right solution is and it may or may not be him." The levels of trust that you obtain entering conversations under this pretense and orientation are levels that many professionals in a sales situation dream of.

Embrace curiosity. This by far has been one of the most practical and effective ways to serve people and acquire raving fans as clients. It keeps you from many of the bad sales behaviors that buyers loathe. It also helps you get a deep understanding of the situation that the buyers are in. Remember earlier how I stated people have a basic need to be heard and understood? Curiosity is the main key to unlocking that experience for a buyer. I've also noticed that with a perspective of curiosity, you tend to not worry about what to say because it makes you more present. You tend to always know what to ask that would reveal important information that helps you and the buyer connect on being the right fit for each other.

Learn how to listen on a deep level. Many people say they are good listeners, but all they do is stop talking without actually listening. Combining listening and curiosity creates a superpower of being able to build a client base of raving fans. Deep levels of listening allow for a differentiated experience for your buyer. When you have the ability to not only get surface-level information, it allows you to get the meaning behind it, and something magical happens. Buyers tell you exactly what to offer to them and how to offer it to them. It's always there to be uncovered. The challenge is most salespeople stop when they get surface-level info because they found a buyer's pain or concern. When you listen at a deep level, you start realizing that the pain or concern is just the starting point of where you have to go. When you dive into the meaning of that pain or concern, buyers start a process of deep trust with you because you are one of the only people to get them.

Make the meetings all about the buyer. You have probably heard this a million times yet experienced yourself talking way too much. The challenge is we are wired to be self-centered. The favorite subject for everyone to talk about is ourselves, and when we are not talking about ourselves, our favorite subject is thinking about ourselves. So, why not utilize this phenomenon to get buyers to tell you everything you need? They are wired to do that, if you just stop focusing on your favorite subject and focus on theirs. Utilizing this and deep listening allows the prospect to make an assessment that you are different compared to the others they interact with in sales situations. When you allow someone to tell you everything you need to know and do it in a differentiated way, you become a valuable partner, not a "service provider."

Align your client-centric words with actions. Many companies and people say that they are client-centric, but then the experience with them is the exact opposite. They talk about themselves and how awesome they are, a lot. They dominate conversations. They ignore the wants and desires of prospects because "they know what their clients need." Their sales process is all about the company or salesperson. You must make the client the center of everything.

Everything you do and how you show up must be aligned. Your offers must be client-centric, your sales process must be client-centric and how you serve must be client-centric.

Listen for promises and make offers into them. When you align with someone's promises, they feel like you are on the same team. Pain and problems are the things blocking prospects from their promises. What prospects are really buying is your help to fulfill promises they made. So, stopping at the pain or problem is only halfway to the most powerful thing to align with. Making an offer to remove a pain is not connected to their strongest desire, but their promises are.

When you make an offer to help someone fulfill a promise, they feel like you are serving them and not selling them. You connect with them on a deeper level because pain or problems are on the surface and promises are below. We all make promises and then try to fulfill them, but few people take the time to assist us in making them come to fruition. Heck, you are reading this book because you are trying to fulfill a promise to yourself, your family, and/or your boss. The pain you have is that you don't feel that your sales mindset is strong enough to fulfill that promise. So, I could say that this book could help remove that pain. On the other hand, I could ask you, "Why does it matter that you remove that pain?" and it's highly likely you will reveal all or a part of a promise you made. It could be: "So I can buy my significant other a house," "So I can hit my quota," or "So I can make one million dollars." Each one of these respectively is a form of promise to your significant other, your boss, and yourself. So, removing the pain is only half of what prospects want to accomplish.

I've seen the approach of serving vs. selling completely transform someone's business and results. Sales becomes something that empowers them to make the impact they desire in other businesses instead of it being a dreaded activity they loath. It takes the unnecessary pressure they put on themselves and gives them the confidence they need to produce the results they are looking for. This approach is also such a natural state for people that they feel more authentic because they don't have to "be a salesperson." So, if you want to either produce more results or stop feeling all the negative things you feel around sales, I encourage you to take on this mindset of serving and watch yourself soar to new heights!

About the Author

Bryan McDonald spent his whole 23-plus-year career in new revenue growth, focused on a superior sales strategy that has a track record of success by serving versus selling people. He's a partner at onPurpose Growth, a coaching and consulting firm that serves entrepreneurs who have ambitious yearly or multi-year revenue goals to actually fulfill that ambition.

Bryan also is the board president of two non-profits. One is a men's Christian leadership development organization called Battel Cry International, helping men become better fathers, leaders, and men. The other is Fox Valley Entrepreneurship Center (FVEC.org), which invests in the growth of local businesses in the suburbs of Chicago. In his free time, Bryan enjoys life with his wife and two daughters.

Email: bmcdonald@onpurposegrowth.com
Website: www.mcdonaldbryan.com

CHAPTER FOURTEEN
THE QUESTION-FOCUSED CONSULTATION

By Brooke Oliphant
Founder, Straight-Up Sales, Orthodontic Growth Consultant
Phoenix, Arizona

Strive not to be a success, but rather to be of value.
—Albert Einstein

My first experience as an entrepreneur began when I was 20 years old.

In the year 2003, the average income for a full-time portrait photographer was 20,000 dollars per year. As the parent of a high school graduate, I can look back on that season of my life and better understand my parents' resistance to my career aspirations. But I was adamant that I was going to be a photographer, and they were adamant that I would graduate from college. The compromise was Colorado Mountain College, where I earned an associate's degree in professional photography.

I was on a mission to make my dreams a reality, carve a unique place for myself in this world, and to prove myself right.

My original dream was to photograph for *National Geographic* and travel the world. That evolved into portraiture after discovering I possessed a natural ability to earn trust and make people feel comfortable in front of my camera. I fell in love with capturing personalities and documenting special moments for others, and my desire to start my own business became my new dream.

After graduation, I returned to my home state, Montana, and quickly opened a portrait studio in a small town a few hours from where I was born and raised. This was the kind of little town that had two stop lights and 7,000 people in the county, where everyone knew everyone, and outsiders needed to prove themselves. I started small and outgrew my first business location in less than a year. It didn't take long before I was able to quit my side jobs and focus full-time on my studio. By my second year I was making over 100,000 dollars. In my mind, I had won at life. I had proven to myself and my closely observing parents that I was capable, living my dream, and being financially independent.

That era of lifestyle, social interaction, and business was different. Maybe every generation has their own "good old days," and while I'm not much for looking backward, there were simplicities and differences worth noting: MySpace was still a thing, Facebook was new, libraries still housed more knowledge than the internet, most businesses didn't have websites, the local newspaper, radio stations, and phone book yellow pages were the only options for advertising, cell phones were still "just phones," PhotoShop was a costly and elite software that was purchased on CD for download, and the war between digital and film photography was raging.

As a 20-something entrepreneur who looked younger than my age, I was often assumed to be a high school employee of "the photographer." Each client interaction began with the uphill battle of proving myself. Looking back, this is where my question-focused, connection-first approach to sales began although at the time I didn't know I was doing anything special or different. I was simply navigating unchangeable circumstances while doing my best to build a great reputation and a successful business.

I knew I was young, so taking offense to the obvious wasn't going to accomplish anything beyond fueling frustration. With a deep desire to prove myself worthy, I approached inquiries and sales conversations by asking questions, and sometimes answering questions with a question until I truly understood what they were looking for. This question-focused style of client interaction invites immediate sharing, and with an understanding of wants and needs, along with valuable information gathered, I was able to present my services as the answer to their desires while highlighting my confidence and authority.

This sales methodology quickly earned trust and resulted in a greater than 90 percent conversion rate from inquiry to paying customers. By my third year as an entrepreneur, I had created a referral-only business with employees and interns, repeat customers, and the need to turn down business.

My growing knowledge of business management, customer service, sales, marketing, and photography led me to get involved in my small-town business community where I pioneered a "shop local" campaign and became the youngest business owner ever elected to the Chamber of Commerce Board of Directors.

My passion for business began to exceed my passion for photography, which came as a huge surprise to me, and my hunger for professional growth eventually led me to expand outside of my local market. I was published, awarded, had earned speaking engagements, and had photographed weddings in numerous states and multiple counties, all by the time I was 25 years old. From the outside looking in, I'd arrived, but I was hungry for greater adventure, growth, and experiences.

My daughter was a toddler when I went through a very public and challenging divorce. My little town felt like a fishbowl and I needed better for myself, my daughter, and our future. Life throws us curve balls, and it's what we do with the events that are outside of our control that matters most. So, I sold my house and my business, said goodbye to dear friends, and moved to Arizona. The need to provide for my little girl motivated my decision making in new and different ways. Being a photographer, simply to hold on to my original vision for my life and career, felt selfish. Yet doing anything other than photography felt like I was giving up and failing.

Over the next 15 years, some lessons I learned quickly and others very slowly. I navigated the highs and lows of being a single parent, experienced another dysfunctional relationship that left me temporarily lost and broken, learned that work can be a happy place that creates stability and belonging when the rest of life feels upside down, and ultimately discovered that the sales style I had developed at my studio could be applied to pediatric dentistry, orthodontics, private practice law, and selling health insurance.

Each business model I've experienced has a different personality of clientele. The structure and flow of each operation is unique. Yet at the foundation, the client/customer/patient needs the same things: connection, understanding, trust, and solutions to a problem, want, or need by working with someone and/ or buying something.

To accomplish this with authenticity and consistency in different industries, personalities of businesses, and as an employee, there were new things I needed to discover and understand about myself. Self-awareness is powerful for transforming yourself from industry average to a rockstar at sales (and life).

With an understanding of myself and a passion for helping others better themselves by providing an undeniably valuable service and experience, I discovered ways to implement my question-focused consultation into the business models of my employers and rediscovered my confidence and love for business.

I believe momentum, either positive or negative, creates more momentum within that energy. I have a daily gratitude practice that supports peak performance in every aspect of my life. I sensor what I consume from social media, television, movies, books, and the news to ensure what I'm feeding my energy and mind supports positivity. I move my body daily and eat a balanced diet that ensures stable energy, quality sleep, and consistently high energy levels. I make lists, set weekly, monthly, quarterly and annual goals, and hold myself accountable. Self-competition is powerful for elevating your professional performance and so is taking responsibility. At the end of the day, this is your life, your career, your sales numbers, and your professional experience… if it isn't good enough, it's your responsibility to take ownership for yourself.

It is also very easy to excel in sales when you have the right mindset, approach, process, skillsets, and methodology. If that sounds like a lot, in some ways you're correct. But in practical application, it's actually more efficient and rewarding work than the traditional "let me try to convince you to buy from me" format. I'll break-it down for you over the next few pages.

In 2019, after a decade of working for others within the dental and orthodontic industries, I founded Straight-Up Sales Orthodontic Coaching and once again stepped into the entrepreneurial world. Before talking about my business, let me tell you a bit about my journey in orthodontics. Orthodontics is a boutique niche within the dental and healthcare world, and it earned a huge and lasting place in my heart from day one. The opportunity for connection with the patients while sharing in a transformative journey is amazing.

When I joined the orthodontic industry in 2014, "sales" was a bad word. The treatment coordinator was expected to sell without selling. The position was trained as a notetaker and info provider on behalf of the doctor and practice, and the expectations for this non-sales sales position were high because the practice's success hinged on prospects saying yes. The industry average conversion rate in orthodontics, both then and now, floats around 50 percent.

I assume it's easy to see that by not calling it a sales position and not training treatment coordinators with sales and boutique customer service skillsets, the poor conversion rates and high turnover rate for this position are understandable.

When I was trained as a treatment coordinator, my initial hurdle was taking intraoral pictures. It became a joke in the office that the "photographer" was struggling to take pictures. For someone who never had an interest in anything medical, putting on gloves and sticking my fingers in someone's mouth seriously stretched me. Beyond learning the foundation and basics of the position, I quickly discovered inefficiencies in the consultation process. Looking at the business model from an entrepreneurial perspective, being a treatment coordinator was a lot of work with a lot of responsibility on behalf of the company, and a 50 percent conversion rate seemed like a bad business model.

I knew that becoming successful in this field required some shifts. Orthodontics calls their prospects "new patients." I quickly reframed this in my mind to "shopper," and while it may seem like semantics, what we name processes and stages within our business model matters. In orthodontics, a shopper must become a buyer before they are a new patient of the practice. With that perspective shift, I started looking at what was said, the format of the consultation, and the overall experience being delivered. Honestly, from an outside perspective, I couldn't blame people for shopping around and trying to negotiate the price. I rarely knew why people left without scheduling to start treatment, and it was because the format of the appointment was heavily scripted and information overloaded. I felt like I was drowning and for a moment thought my previous successes were simply luck. It can be challenging as an employee to positively influence your position, especially if you've been instructed to do everything in a specific way under a micromanagement style.

Fast forward a couple of years, and under the leadership of a growth-focused orthodontist in a season of professional reinvention, I was given the opportunity to apply my question-focused sales methodology to the new patient consultation. It was within this experience that I discovered my approach to communication and sales, which had earned me significant success as a portrait photographer, also applied to orthodontics. As a treatment coordinator with a drive to exceed expectations and an entrepreneurial ownership over my position, the doctor I worked for was able to experience, over and over, the highest production in practice history. As an established business of more than 20 years with a great reputation, the financial growth exceeded expectations and created opportunities to expand in ways that weren't possible at "industry average." I earned industry recognition as a top-converting sales professional with the highest accolade for same-day contracts.

At the foundation of every sales position is the need to win often and consistently. Each business model that I've personally experienced, along with countless others that I've been exposed to and influenced as a consultant, has shown me that my formula for question-focused sales, where relationships and connection matter first, can be applied across most industries.

In each of my professional experiences, I discovered that caring deeply about how my service or product could benefit others created a foundation for earning trust, solving problems, and creating a sales process that was for my client, instead of about myself. If you're worried about being "salesy" it's because what you're doing or the way you're interacting with your clients is about you, not them. To change this, operate from a question-focused sales philosophy by doing the following:

- Asking more questions
- Caring deeply
- Identifying the problem your service or product solves, and then learning about each of your customers individually

The question-focused sales approach requires passion, knowledge, confidence, and a willingness to go above and beyond for your customers. If you want your sales process to be about you and what you have to sell more than about connection and delivering an experience that creates value for your shopper, maybe this method isn't for you.

In orthodontics, earning trust that results in a same-day conversion rate greater than 80 percent requires treating the entire person, not just their teeth. By understanding the problems, dreams, and values of each customer's transformation, you are able to guide them toward decision making by solving their needs with your service. Therefore, your emotional intelligence as a sales professional is one of your superpowers.

As a sales coach for orthodontic treatment coordinators, we go on a journey together that identifies limiting beliefs and self-sabotaging actions while also closely evaluating the sales experience for inefficiencies that are reducing sales success. Designing and implementing a new patient experience that's intended to guide decision making, answer questions, invite sharing, earn trust, and give the prospect a clear path forward requires you to care deeply about your company, team, service, shopper, and yourself. While that may seem obvious, I'm sure we can all agree that most business models, if closely evaluated, are designed to service the business's needs more than the customers' needs. For those businesses that stand the test of time, processes do start to age and become inefficient because making changes requires effort, planning, and action that challenges our comfort zones. Therefore, peak performance sales success also requires a growth mindset and the willingness to evolve within an industry, economy, and society that's forever-changing.

With over two decades of practicing and implementing my question-focused consultation, and now teaching others how to make it their own, these are some of the key benefits to adopting this sales methodology:

- You will create raving fans from day one.
- Your work ethic and connection with your customers will become your personal brand.
- Your sales wins will be authentic and your sales losses will be educational.
- You will know what matters to your customers and be able to quickly evolve to meet and exceed their expectations.
- You will discover who your ideal customers are and who you don't want to work with.
- Your success will become limitless, only capped by your desired lifestyle or the pre-designed capacity of your business.
- Your work will be rewarding, elevating your human experiences both professionally and personally.

With a willingness to innovate, combined with a desire to continuously improve, the question-focused sales approach facilitates your peak performance experiences to compound into a lifestyle that's rich with connection, value, positive impact, and financial success, the kind of winning that makes the world a better place.

About the Author

Brooke Oliphant is the founder of Straight-Up Sales Orthodontic Coaching. She coaches clients all over the United States on how to "better their best" by improving their new patient experience and implementing her question-focused consultation sales methodology, which aligns with her mission to bless the lives of others and make the world a better place. She is an avid reader, enjoys traveling and nature, is a fitness enthusiast, and loves to cook. Creating memories with her family and being an actively involved mom were motivations to create a home-based company that services clients remotely. Brooke is a public speaker and teacher, offering industry-specific insight and motivation to inspire orthodontists and treatment coordinators to take action that will elevate their professional experience and financial success by better serving the needs of their patients.

To learn more from Brooke and to discuss private coaching and speaking opportunities, connect with her at www.straightupsales.com.

CHAPTER FIFTEEN

EMPOWER SALES TEAMS WITH 80:20 TRANSFORMATION

By Michel Privé
Outsourced VP of Sales, Growth Strategist
Cypress, Texas

*You don't get results by focusing on the results. You get results
by focusing on the actions that produce results.*
—Mike Hawkins

The Why

A few years ago, a prominent company hired me to merge the sales teams of two competing business units (BU). More than 85 percent of the BUs' revenue was derived from one industry sector. This sector was hot for four quarters and collapsed in the second year. Due to the demand for BUs' products in other segments, we had an opportunity to grow sales and reduce the risk for the business. The newly merged business unit needed a leader to deliver the necessary work. My duties in this capacity were to:

1. Diversify the business
2. Grow above both the market rate and the expected corporation target
3. Build a sales team with the right team members for the future
4. Implement tools and structure to allow scalability and repeatability
5. Reorganize the sales department to meet all the above criteria

After six quarters, we met the objectives of points one to five. All parties were happy on the surface. Meanwhile, a silent storm was brewing in the shadow of our success. Over the last few quarters, we have seen our clients' key performance indicators (KPIs) going down towards the lowest 80 percent and our lead time becoming one of the longest in our commodity segment. My sales team was getting irritated and unmotivated as they needed help hitting bonus targets.

A few minutes before a scheduled corporate management call, we lost a critical order worth $300K from one of our best clients. The only reasons expressed by the clients were the lead time and declining KPI to deliver on time.

During this management call, I looked at our backlog to see what could explain this situation. When it was time to report my team's activity, I realized the $300K order composed of 18-part numbers was lost because of the lead time created by about $300K worth of a hundred separate orders, each with a quantity of one.

By focusing on the task, I realized our customer base and order acceptance practices were why our rapid growth without boundaries created this harmful situation. The more we grew, the more our clients suffered, including the most important ones, to our long-term success.

The Pain – Lack of Room to Grow	The Solution : Make room to grow
• Unrealistic/Unachievable factory lead times	• Concentrate efforts and energy on core business
• Inability to execute current business plan	• Focus only on top product lines
• Failure in providing Best Customer Service	• Grow EBIT orders and dollars
• Inability to introduce new Products	• Increase overall market and specific customers

The Who

While salespeople always look at their clients, it may be from different perspectives.

- The *hunter's* favorite quote is: "It is a number game, and the next one will buy."
- The *farmer's* favorite quote is: "They renewed for another year."

Salespeople are loathe to:

- Deliver bad news to their clients
- Lose
- Say no and hate being in the position to have to do so

They protect their professional and personal reputations and fight to keep them perfect. They have a long-term relationship with their clients. They go out of their way to convert a prospect and deliver what their new client seeks.

With all this in mind, for the next six consecutive months, I asked my sales team to do the opposite of what they felt they were both born to and loved doing. We worked together with their trust in our leadership team and the project itself, and stimulated their willingness to expose their reputations to execute the plan. In so doing, we made an incredible business transformation.

It's a tale of a sales-led project changed from a low earnings before interest, taxes, and amortization (EBITDA) business to a fast-growing, profitable, and competitive winning machine.

We needed a transformation turnaround based on Pareto's 80:20 principles. For it to be executed smoothly for the clients, it needed to be led by us—the sales department.

The What

A plan was put in place which lined up all parties and the benefits they would gain from engaging in this crusade. With the BU general manager (GM), we prepared projections of the program's potential short-term *negative* implications. These ranged from:

- Possible revenue loss and reduction of clients on the tangible and intangible sides
- The potential loss of important clients or salespersons
- Potential internal and external tension
- Damaged company reputation in the marketplace

At the same time, the following *positive* mid- to long-term effects were anticipated:

- Increased good clients' KPI
- Reduced lead times (to quote, to enter a PO, to get engineering to deliver, to manufacture, to get paid)
- Reduced number of transactions
- Improved EBITDA

- Reduced sales cycle, with a focus on the right prospects, clients, and business segments

To execute this plan, the sales team needed to receive a generous bonus and to do a lot of counter-intuitive tasks during the transition period. In addition, a new tracking method needed to be established. This involved:

- Tracking the dollar value per transaction ($/T), measured and reported weekly by the inside sales manager
- Developing sets of criteria to measure our overall progress

Eleven percent of our total business was with our sister division BUs, all in quadrant 4 (see table 1).

Working with the BU GM, we prepared and presented our project to the division management, along with the pros/cons, and the new sales incentive program. This was done to avoid anticipated resistance to proposed changes.

As an additional challenge, some of our frustrated small BU customers were also large and powerful clients of the parent corporation. We wanted the board to know this information, as the market could paint the corporation with a bad reputation if we failed to deliver and upset clients with our BU program restructuring. We received positive reviews and advice to get the plan ready for approval by the board. This approval happened, and we received their permission to proceed.

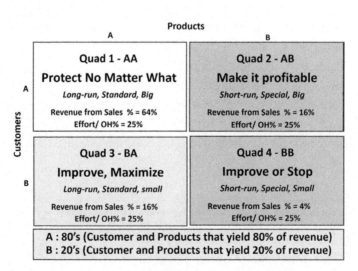

Table 1

Rule #1 of 80:20—Refrain from Breaking Anything You Are Unable to Repair

From the data point of view, we knew at this stage:

- Who were our profitable clients
- Who were those that cost us
- Who were the ones wasting our time
- Who were those with whom we needed to invest more of our time

Under confidentiality, this analysis was presented to our inside and outside sales managers to get their plan and approach "buy-in." The following detailed presentation was shared with them, highlighting:

- Client benefits (clients' pain/sales team's pain to go away)
- Sales team member benefits (new bonus scheme indexed on EBITA)
- New business increase tools and techniques
- The better services and processes that enable us to work more efficiently

With the numbers analysis to back it up, the overall deal was nailed. The following details were precisely presented:

- What was going to happen and how
- Who would do what within the plan
- Tactics to be used with unhappy clients
- The internal and external training required
- The total commitment from operations to give all involved concerning what was wanted

Some of the specifics include quotes being available in three days; engineering completed in one week; delivery in six to eight weeks; all customer KPI >95 percent; and the excellent bonus scheme to pay both the individual and the sales team performance.

Rule #2 of 80:20—Get Everyone Onboard: Same Direction, Same Speed, Same Language

Still under confidentiality, the sales managers and our team validated the results the numerical analysis revealed. Together, we established the critical KPIs to track the smooth and efficient deployment and accountability of all the sales team members, including ourselves.

An online customer service training course was chosen to train all our sales employees in efficiently handling unhappy customers. Once this customer service training program was completed, our sales team leaders ironed out their specific plan details.

We then presented this action plan and its implementation tactics to the entire sales team, including all aspects of the program. The sales team individuals now knew their specific KPIs, which included their expected:

- $/T targets for their clients
- Quote conversion rate
- Long-term agreement target
- New leads and customer acquisition targets
- New product placement targets

The sales team then "signed onto" their new compensation plan, validating that they understood what we expected from them. Other departments also had their targets provided by sales and approved by operations. These included the quoting, engineering, manufacturing, QA, contract, legal, accounting, and HR departments' outcome-specific goals.

The program was launched at the end of December. Taking charge of the internal customers (as they were the most challenging of the groups), I personally oversaw the activities of two inside salespeople and became the "front man" to implement the necessary changes at our sister companies.

As expected, we encountered resistance from my internal customer's peers and found it to be a difficult six months.

The How

We started by sending letters to our clients. Below are some examples of specific phrases used in these correspondences:

- Your next PO needs to meet the following minimum dollar value per line and a new minimum order quantity.
- Prices for this item need to be re-quoted.
- Lead times for these items are being changed from XX to YY.
- We are increasing our investment in providing *you* with the best customer service available.
- Here is/are the product(s)/service(s) we are providing for free, starting next quarter.

After two weeks of intensive communication, each team member knew how to prioritize clients with either a management visit, video call, email, or simple phone call.

The BU GM, my sales managers, and I were all "on call" to immediately support any difficult discussion our sales team members had to make with or involving any of their clients. These included "anytime" conversations with either sales team members or their clients, explaining the benefit to/for both parties to improve how we now conducted business.

The sales team members discovered how to drive their discussions. After four intense weeks, the dust settled, and we started to see the quadrant 1, 2, and 3 clients making their move to improve their $/T.

Execution: Month 1—Salespeople Drama

Nervous about the potential negative outcome implications of the project, quadrants 1, 2, 3, or 4 client discussions started. There was drama with our salespeople. They disliked this period of informing clients about our transformation and what it meant to them. We experienced the full spectrum of attitudes from sales team individuals towards the program. These ranged from very scared and skeptical to very motivated and engaged in harvesting the expected outcome.

80:20 Execution: Month 2—Salespeople Stress

Strict rules of doing business were put in place. Minimum order quantities or dollar value, and minimum quantity per line orders imposed to clients came along with benefits for our clients. Clients welcomed these benefits (stock availability, shorter lead time, five-star service access, daily delivery reports, and weekly stock reports). These were all services previously unavailable from us. Our sales hunters worked from stricter new sets of criteria to add new business; They focused on targeting only specific types of business where the $/T was above the average.

80:20 Execution: Month 3 to 5— Salespeople Relief and Smiles

The sales team received their first post-project introduction bonuses. The "hunter team" saw the benefit of their individual hard work. The quadrant 1 and 2 clients were actively participating in the project. Our "farmer team" was making progress with their clients, providing excellent customer services—focusing on the benefits for these clients. The original quadrant 4 clients either left us completely or became quadrant 2 or 3 clients.

Happier clients + Less Work + Bonus Paid =
Happy, Efficient, Motivated Salespeople

80:20 Execution: Month 6—Salespeople's Pride and Joy

All sales team members started to make substantial quarterly bonuses (most doubled their salaries). Each salesperson knew which of their levers to pull to win profitable business. The key account managers (our farmer team) started to both win additional market share and sell new products and services to their clients, thanks to the best KPI in the industry.

Clients began to give us referrals, thereby enabling our hunter team to win great profitable business away from the competition. The workload to support existing clients was reduced, thereby allowing expanded bandwidth for the team to prospect and hunt in adjacent markets. Our new KPIs allowed us to fast-track development to market industries we previously could not handle. By focusing on winning the right business from our competitors, we grew our quadrant 1 and 2 clients.

Our client base grew from 80:20 to 95:5. These five
were the new clients in the prototype stage.

80:20—The Outcome

At the end of Q1, the BU reported a five percent EBITDA growth to the board. Additionally, sales grew above both the plan and forecast. Our initial $/T doubled, with no fundamental changes in lead time or KPIs.

At the end of Q2:

- Our EBITDA grew another six percent, a cumulative 13 percent since the program's inception.
- Bookings/billing/backlog (BBB) value and ratio grew above plan and expectation.
- Our original $/T was multiplied by 2.5.
- We started to see a lead time reduction in quoting, engineering, and manufacturing for some product lines and services.
- Our quadrants 1, 2, and 3 clients' KPI moved above 90 percent. They were happy—receiving the customer service they truly deserved.

At the end of Q3:

- Our $/T tripled, and sales grew 15 percent over the previous quarter, far above plan.
- Our EBITDA rose 16 percent in ten months.
- Our top 20 large accounts' KPIs were all above 95 percent.
- All the departments met their targets.
- Our deal conversion rate moved from 65 percent to 95 percent for existing clients and from ten percent to 50 percent for new prospects.

During these initial three quarters, most sales team members doubled their compensation in bonuses. The other departments did very well too. We were now working efficiently, smartly, smoothly, and peacefully.

The board saw this transformation happening under their eyes:

- After the first quarter results, which validated the plan worked, they started to investigate and review the key indicators of all their BUs.
- At the end of Q2, armed with our additional EBITDA progression, they asked the other BUs to start building their own 80:20 plan.
- At the end of Q3, the other BUs launched their projects.

- At the end of Q4, our BU's EBITDA grew by 19 percent; sales grew by 21 percent.

In 12 months, our BU reputation moved from okay, to improved for most and terrible (internal clients) for some, to great for most clients and fantastic for others. In the end, we won several large profitable clients from our competitors. We became:

- The technology partners for our commodity for these large customers, involved in the early and every design stage of their product development
- Gained "first right to refuse" status in developing products or technology to help them win market shares
- Their solid partners

Rule #3 of 80:20: You Can Only Win with a Solid Collaborative Team

Armed with these new tactical tools, we supported colleagues in delivering our sales-led 80:20 program before their new ERP implementation at five of my other business units. Thanks to a well-executed 80:20 plan, these implementations went smoothly for our clients, employees, and suppliers.

Conclusion

When you have the following, implementing a successful 80:20 program becomes so much easier:

- Planning and preparation
- Clarity and detailed tasks for each of the actors
- Commitment from each of the actors
- A fair compensation plan based on the program's outcome
- Clients in sight at every stage

The other company division's BUs implemented their 80:20 program, led by the management/operations and finance personnel, and integrated it into their sales organizations. Unfortunately, this failed to go well. During their process, they lost clients, salespeople, and employees, and implementation took far longer than required. They eventually recovered.

All this goes to show that the necessary sensibility to delight clients and conviction skills required to communicate the benefit of the changes to clients, salespeople, and colleagues are crucial to a well-executed plan.

When sales leaders are adequately equipped with these skills, effectively using them leads to a successful 80:20, a successful corporate machine, and a successful achievement.

About the Author

Focused on the sales process and execution, Michel Privé is an accomplished, dynamic executive with 25-plus years of experience successfully leading diverse organizations providing products and services.

Today, acting as an outsourced VP of sales consultant, Michel hires salespeople, directs, and grows companies at a two-digit rate, whether they small businesses or 100-million-dollar organizations. His proven track record of establishing compelling visions, effective sales strategies, and building teams to achieve profitable growth makes him the leader to meet *your* needs and requirements.

Email: mprive@salesxceleration.com
Website: www.slictexas.com

CHAPTER SIXTEEN

THE POWER OF PEOPLE-CENTRIC LEADERSHIP

By Laetitia Ribier-Costa
Outsourced VP Sales; Start-up & Scale-up Advisor
Porto, Portugal

Wherever there is a human being, we have an opportunity for kindness.
—Seneca

In the world of sales, it is common for promotion to occur internally, benefiting individual contributors who have started developing skills in leadership (sometimes) or maybe have been top performers (often). However, not all companies provide a safe space for newly appointed sales managers to develop skills and grow further. Most of these first-time managers are just thrown out into the arena, asking them to manage and lead a team of seven, eight, or maybe 15 or more salespeople without having a clue about what it means to be a good manager of people.

Some companies have a managers development program specifically built by their learning and development team, ensuring the new managers are well assisted in learning their new roles before jumping into it and crushing their team targets with a high team spirit. For those who have not had this type of support—don't be shy, it happens a lot. I'd like to give my two cents about what I have learned so far in my career in sales, both as an individual contributor and a manager.

But first, let me take you back some years behind, when I first started my professional career. At that time, I did not get the support I should have had as a junior saleswoman, and as a result, my willingness to stay in sales was actually jeopardized. I was pondering whether I should keep going onto this path. "Maybe sales is not for me after all?" I thought.

Even though I liked building relationships with my prospects and clients, and the challenges involved in crushing targets, I couldn't help but feel like a terrible salesperson. However, I kept pursuing my career in sales, without huge conviction, but hey, it paid well and there were a lot of opportunities. And I did well. A few years later, I was lucky enough to join the company of my dream—LinkedIn—and to discover a whole new world of management, a compassionate management. This is the type of management that makes you grow; that makes you become who you should have been since the beginning. You are more authentic, true to yourself. You are less afraid of speaking up. You are empowered; you can make mistakes and learn from them. You feel you are developing at a higher speed than you did previously. You gain confidence; you gain knowledge; you gain courage. And suddenly, you even enjoy sales and see all its potential! As a result—you become a better sales performer.

Have you ever yourself taken the time to reflect on which circumstance you were the most productive in your job? If so—or if you're doing this right now—I'm pretty sure that if you picture the manager you had at the time, it was someone empathetic and thoughtful. I don't mean lax. You don't want a manager that doesn't lead or who agrees with everything and never challenges you, but they were probably supportive.

Of course, there are other factors in a salesperson's success: what skills you bring to the table, your mindset, your level of confidence, your resilience, how targets are set up, the product or services being sold, the go-to-market strategy set up, and so on. But let's say the stars are aligned, and on top of that, you are working with a manager who empowers you, who believes in you, who helps you take the best out of yourself but still coaches you on areas you need to improve. This is someone who supports you as well, who removes barriers for you to perform in your job, who listens to you and takes actions afterwards. With this, you have the perfect recipe for success, for I maintain that *kindness is at the heart of success.*

If you are a first-time manager, or if you've been in sales management for a bit and are struggling with your team's achievement, there are some principles that you can apply to build a winning sales team that performs at its best, keeping in mind the first principle of all: do things with heart. Be kind to yourself, be kind to others.

Express Your Vision

Expressing your vision to your team is extremely important. I'm not talking here about the vision or mission of the company. Though that should be aligned with them too. Rather, you should make it clear to your team what you aim to achieve as a group and how it will contribute to the wider company vision. You need to communicate relentlessly about this and build a plan to execute that vision.

A best practice is to build it together with your team during a workshop, to engage people more in visualizing that statement of purpose and building the path to success, and to create a story around it, so people will easily remember it. However, let each person decide on how they will achieve that vision, and keep monitoring with them, individually (one-on-one) or collectively (during team meetings), to ensure everyone knows where they are at in terms of building that vision. What is important here is to verify one by one that it is clear for them how their results and successes will contribute to reaching your team goal. There is no better moment to do that than during a weekly one-on-one, where you can check the message has been well received and see how each individual feels about it on an ongoing basis.

Use your weekly huddles or team-building events to reinforce the message as well. Talk about it, show images to make it more visual (diagrams, charts). Keep it brief though. You don't want people to feel overwhelmed or lose interest in the topic.

If you are a director, make sure your direct managers have perceived the point, communicate clearly about it, and regularly monitor. You can also use a quarterly one-on-one with their direct reports to guarantee the good reception and understanding of it.

Have a Clear Plan to Execute

When sales reps look only at their ultimate goal, there are chances this objective is quite big. Whether it is a financial target, a target on number of calls performed, or a target on how many products they need to sell. Whether they are monthly, quarterly, or annually—it will feel bigger. Looking at a goal to attain can often feel overwhelming, especially if people lack a good enough pipeline and are struggling to understand how on Earth they'll be able to achieve it.

As a manager, you can provide guidance and ask them to start dividing this goal into smaller goals, smaller steps that they need to take to attain it. Then, chances are they will see more easily that it should be manageable. If they have a yearly target, help them to divide it into a quarter and then into weeks. Even for a long sales cycle, like Enterprise sales, there is a way to plan all actions needed to take in order to be successful. By planning it, sales reps have more control over the sales cycle and they can accelerate the closing.

And most importantly, they can start planning what actions they need to take in order to turn the small steps into something realistic. If they still feel this is too much, they would need to play with other parameters such as increasing their average size deals or accelerating their time to close deals (and think about what actions they need to take in order to do so).

One way to avoid feeling overwhelmed and become a top performer is to always be one step ahead of what is necessary to attain, month after month, quarter after quarter. If your direct reports start working less, rest on their laurels, or become over-confident thanks to the pipeline they have, they need to be aware they will use this advance they had, and at some point in their journey they will struggle again to reach their targets.

As a manager, having the ability to generate a winning mindset for your sales reps is crucial. Hence, to come back to my previous comment, this is also central to ensure your people feel powerful, confident, secure, and supported in their ambitions. Again, managing people with care will definitely increase your ability to get this successful mindset. And for that, there are some tools or systems you can use, on top of kindness and empathy.

Build the Team You Dream

As a leader, you don't have control over everything. Some part of your job is just influencing others. Some part of your job is just accepting the status quo and moving forward. There is one thing though you can almost entirely have control in building up: your team. Use that power to its utmost extent!

First, you hire your people (directly or indirectly), meaning you can ensure some criteria in building a winning team will be met such as a diversity of background, of culture, of race, of disability, of age, of gender, of family status, and so on. Having a complementary team is what brings the possibilities to over-achieve. When you have diverse people, you have different opinions, different skillsets, and different mindsets. All of them together will have the brightest ideas possible to keep growing the business.

As a manager, you also are the one in possession of the strategy to drive the business further. Specifically, there is something you can do to help drive the business: set up specific routines to ensure your team has the habit of always bringing new leads (and then deals) within their pipeline. Use a bit of gamification to add fun because it's not easy to be 100 percent of the time focused on the business.

I have experienced first-hand sales reps who were focusing too much on their top deals, forgetting about the long tail of their pipeline and the quick wins they could have at the end of the quarter. This is your duty as a manager to ensure it will not happen. You need to provide guidelines through a tight management of your direct reports pipeline during one-on-one: review current deals, challenges, blockers, and unexpected events; and ask questions to make them realize they might have only a small percentage of information to finalize the deal in the end. Never rely entirely on what someone is telling you; like every human being, salespeople have blind spots.

There is absolutely no need for finger-pointing though (and that's not my point here), but asking the right questions in coaching mode will allow someone to realize by themselves they lack answers, they lack information, and so they need to go back to their clients to get these answers.

Keep Being Your Team's Cheerleader

As a manager, be a cheerleader. All along the journey of a salesperson, there are highs and lows. People will be overjoyed when closing a deal. Especially if they were expecting it so much, but the deal kept being pushed away, and they got themselves to the finish line. Or the deals they have spent hours brainstorming to convert, the ones that were almost hypothetical a few weeks ago and turned out to be their biggest bet thanks to their work.

But also, they will be disappointed, anxious, angry, and lost when they won't be able to reach their goal despite the long hours and hard work. Sometimes working hard does not automatically equal success. Working well is what matters. The role of a leader is so crucial when these moments happen. A manager is both the coach and cheerleader of the team. The person that will help them overcome these obstacles.

Coaching someone first means you are able to recognize when they are not going down the right path, so you guide that person, step by step, question after question, towards the victory path. Making someone realize they might have been spending time towards tasks that did not bring value is the best gift a coach-manager can give. It can happen through constructive feedback as well when sales reps are really blind about their actions.

But sales reps also need their manager to be their cheerleader—and notice here there is the word "leader" within "cheerleader." Why is this so important?

First of all, because we all like to get praised for our job, it makes us feel better, but also because it creates a deeper interconnection—"My manager is seeing the efforts I have been putting into this, even though I was not successful." Encouraging people all along their journey is much more beneficial, but also very underrated. We tend to recognize people only once they have accomplished something.

What happens when someone shows some appreciation for the work you are doing towards success before you actually achieve your goals? You are filled with joy, you are more confident, you are more creative, you step out of your comfort zone more easily, and in the end, you have a greater triumph than you would have if your path to it had been broken by lack of clarity, unconfident thoughts, and anxiety.

As you know, one way to help people feel good as an individual in a team of people is to practice regular recognition through rewards, official recognition, or even personal thank-you notes. Don't limit those rewards and acknowledgements only to those who are over-achieving. Find ways to celebrate all your team members. Celebration does not have to be only directed to your top performers.

Of course, the twin to that practice is not to start recognizing people that have not even tried to be successful or to grant rewards to people all the same way. There is something special about your top achievers, and you need to make them keep feeling they are special. You want them to keep investing in the business, in your team. You have to have the right balance here. Build team cohesion.

There is no better feeling than when we feel "at home." Where we feel we can be authentic, our true self, with the people we spend most of our time with—our colleagues. For that, the role of the manager is also decisive. How this manager makes everyone feel in the team will have undoubtedly a huge effect on the well-being of every team member.

Starting with giving a seat to everyone at the table. You will most probably have a mixed team of extroverted and introverted people. The extroverted will always be happy to share their ideas, to comment, and to challenge other people in the room. The introverted, on the other hand, will most likely keep quiet. It does not mean they don't have excellent ideas or comments. They are just not comfortable sharing them in public. Take the time to talk to them afterwards, in a one-on-one, once the team meeting or brainstorming session is over. You can be surprised how introverted people can see details others don't.

Also essential in any team is the power of activities out of the corporate world. People bond differently when they are not in a professional environment. When you want to celebrate your team's accomplishments, take them to a nice restaurant of their choice or a team-building activity that pleases the majority of them, and go to the places where the minority would like to go too

To finish, I would like to circle back to my previous point—be kind to yourself. It all starts with us. As human beings, who are we towards ourselves? Am I indulgent to my mistakes? Am I fine with my flaws? Am I enjoying my learning journey?

We set examples to others when we are leaders. Our actions and attitudes will help our team to follow the same principles we apply to ourselves. And nothing is more important to winning or being successful than the way that led us towards that. Be proud of how we have been able to grow, how we cope with adversity, how we have developed resilience, and how we turned out to be stronger after a defeat.

Step by step, day after day, let's be kind to ourselves as we continue to grow as salespeople and lead others toward becoming the best salespeople they can be.

About the Author

Laetitia Ribier-Costa is an independent Sales Operating Partner working alongside start-ups & scale-ups backed by VC and PE, mainly in the Saas and Tech industries, to help them grow better (and faster) by structuring their revenue organization, accelerate their performance and excel in people management. She formerly served as a Regional Sales Manager at LinkedIn.

Laetitia holds a Master Degree in Law and in International Management, and is also a certified coach in Personal, Leadership and Executive Coaching from Kingstown College. Originally from France, she has lived in different countries throughout her career and is currently living in Portugal with her family.

Email : laetitia@revenue-in.com
Website : revenue-in.com
LinkedIn: www.linkedin.com/in/laetitiaribier/

CHAPTER SEVENTEEN
SALES, MINDSET, AND NEUROSCIENCE

By Tim Robertson
Sales & Growth Accelerator, Tech Consultant
London, England, United Kingdom

Success in sales is 80 percent mindset and 20 percent skillset. Your beliefs,
attitudes, and outlook determine your altitude in the world of sales.
—Brian Tracy

Anyone who has worked in the pharmaceutical sales sector is aware of the problems of seeing general practitioners and hospital consultants, especially when some of them refuse to see you for two years!

I recall one time having a particularly difficult day early on in my prior career in pharmaceutical sales. I had spent the entire day calling clinics, departments, and surgeons, but no one seemed interested in scheduling appointments with me. I began to feel disappointed and wondered if I was even in the right field. But then I remembered the importance of positive thinking from my coaching and development manager (they had them back then too!), and I decided to take a new approach.

Instead of feeling defeated, I took a pause to practice some mindfulness at his suggestion. I concentrated on my breathing and told myself positive affirmations, such as, "I am successful, and I can do this." I also imagined myself making effective sales calls and booking appointments.

I decided to give it another go. I picked up the phone and called potential general practice surgeries and hospitals again to schedule appointments. To my astonishment, I was able to schedule many successful sales calls in a succession. I felt considerably more upbeat and accomplished towards the end of the day than I had before.

That incident taught me the value of mindset.

There is a school of thinking that our ideas and attitudes as salespeople can have a significant impact on our level of sales success. Neuroscience has shed light on the different ways in which our brain can influence our thoughts and can either hinder or enhance our performance.

Let's look into the relationship between mindset and sales performance and focus on the neuroscientific roots of this relationship. Furthermore, we will also look at the various ways of thinking and the methods that may be utilised to change them in order to increase our sales success, as much research has demonstrated that a person's frame of mind can have a big effect on their brain, which in turn can affect the individual's level of success in sales.

Most people can be classed as having a fixed mindset or a growth mindset when it comes to their mental state. These are the two main categories. A fixed mindset occurs when an individual believes that their abilities are unchangeable and cannot evolve over time. People with a fixed mindset may believe that their success or failure is predetermined and that they have no control over it. These people may also assume there is nothing they can do to improve their situation. They may also be prone to believing that the success or failure of others is predetermined. This kind of thinking can lead to a fear of failure as well as a lack of enthusiasm to attempt new things or take risks, all of which can be detrimental to a sales success.

A growth mindset, on the other hand, is the belief that our abilities may be enhanced via consistent work and focus on a certain job. People with a growth mindset view failures as opportunities to learn and progress; as a result, they are more willing to take measured risks and attempt new things than people who do not have a growth mindset. This attitude of mind can lead to increased resiliency, adaptability, and motivation, all of which can contribute to increased sales performance.

Individuals with a growth mindset have more active neural connections in the prefrontal cortex, the part of the brain involved in executive functions such as decision-making, problem solving, and attention, according to research. This demonstrates that those with a growth mindset are better able to handle the demands of the sales sector, which requires quick thinking, problem solving, and flexibility from its practitioners.

A study conducted by the University of Pennsylvania discovered that salespeople with a growth mindset outperformed those with the view that their abilities are set in stone and cannot be improved. The concept that our abilities can be learned and developed through hard work and dedication was termed as the growth mindset. The study's findings revealed that people with a growth mindset had higher levels of resiliency, adaptability, and willingness to learn and develop, which led to higher levels of sales success.

Another study, conducted by the University of Toronto, discovered that sales professionals with a positive mindset, or the belief that they are capable of success, were more likely to engage in proactive selling behaviours, such as seeking out new opportunities and networking, than those with a negative mindset, or the belief that they are unlikely to succeed. This was in comparison to sales professionals who had a negative outlook and believed they were unlikely to succeed. The study found that persons with a positive outlook had higher levels of self-efficacy, or belief in their ability to succeed. Furthermore, these individuals were more eager to take risks and attempt new things, which resulted in higher sales success.

Furthermore, some research has shown that having a positive way of thinking can affect the brain's reward system, which in turn can affect our behaviour. According to the findings of a study conducted by the University of Michigan, people who had an optimistic outlook had higher levels of dopamine, a neurotransmitter associated with reward and motivation. This demonstrates that persons with a positive outlook are more likely to be motivated to engage in sales behaviours like cold calling and prospecting, which can lead to better sales performance.

When it comes to sales performance, some researchers believe that having a positive mindset is critical to success. According to research, neurology of the brain has an important part in forming our thinking and behaviour. Dr. John Medina, a molecular biologist and author of the book *Brain Rules*, believes that "emotions are the gatekeepers to learning." This means that our emotional state can either hurt or help us learn and perform successfully.

Taking this a step further, neuroscientist Paul D. MacLean proposed the triadic brain theory, which states that the human brain is divided into three distinct sections.

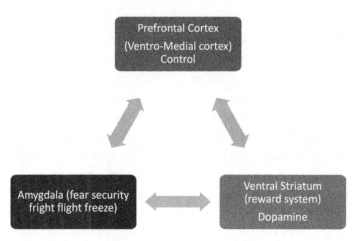

The Triadic Brain - Adapted from Ernst Hardin and Pine 2006

The limbic system includes the amygdala. It is the emotional centre of the brain and has a significant impact on your frame of mind. A pessimistic outlook can activate the amygdala, causing fight-or-flight reactions that might impair decision-making and creativity. A positive outlook, on the other hand, can keep the amygdala in check and assist in minimising stress and anxiety, allowing you to think more clearly and creatively. Genetics, early-life experiences, epigenetics, and environmental factors all influence the size and function of the amygdala.

Fear conditioning can help us recover from rejection or setbacks. The *Harvard Business Review* records that increasing emotional intelligence—including the amygdala's emotion-regulating abilities—resulted in a 20 percent increase in sales effectiveness.

While emotional intelligence and stress and anxiety management are crucial abilities for us, it is vital to remember that emotional regulation and resilience are complicated processes involving various brain regions and psychological elements. For example, the prefrontal cortex is important in emotion regulation and decision-making, and mindfulness practices which have been found to be useful in lowering anxiety and stress.

The prefrontal cortex (PFC), or more specifically the ventro-medial prefrontal cortex part of the neocortex, is like the command-and-control centre for peak sales performance. It's where crucial abilities like decision-making, problem solving, planning, and cognitive flexibility come into play. To excel in sales, we must have a healthy PFC to keep us sharp and alert. One of the

PFC's superpowers is its capacity to maintain attention and concentration. We can stay on track and complete our tasks efficiently if our PFC is healthy.

The PFC also assists us in controlling our emotions and urges. A functioning PFC ensures that we remain rational and reasonable. Furthermore, the PFC is critical for cognitive flexibility, which is the ability to adjust to new conditions and methods. When things change, those who can't bend may struggle. They can, however, adapt and thrive in the presence of a healthy PFC.

Finally, the PFC is involved in working memory. We must recall customer requirements, product attributes, and sales data. A healthy PFC allows us to keep all of that information on hand and ready to use in our sales endeavours. In short, the PFC is critical for developing a positive mindset that leads to peak sales performance. It assists us in remaining focused, managing emotions, remaining adaptable, and keeping critical information at our fingertips.

Lastly the ventral striatum (and a part called the nucleus accumbens) functions similarly to the reward centre of the brain. It is in charge of controlling motivation and reinforcing behaviours connected with pleasure or reward. As a result, it can assist you in being motivated and persistent in achieving sales targets and exploring new prospects for success.

As a result, any of us who want to achieve our highest potential should cultivate a positive, growth-oriented mindset. This can be accomplished by activating the brain in a variety of ways, including visualisation, positive affirmations, and mindfulness practices.

Visualisation is a strong skill that can assist us in creating mental images of ourselves accomplishing our objectives. According to research, visualising achievement engages the same brain regions as experiencing success, which can help reinforce good thoughts and behaviours.

Positive affirmations are remarks that support our positive self-image. We can improve our self-image and establish a growth mindset by repeating positive affirmations. We begin by affirming ourselves, like an inner self-talk about how we are able to carry out and deal with whatever comes our direction.

Meditation and deep breathing are two mindfulness practices that can assist us to reduce stress and enhance our emotional management. We can think more clearly and perform better when we are less stressed.

Finally, the triadic brain theory proposes that the triadic brain plays an important role in molding our thinking and behaviour, which is critical for us to achieve peak performance.

So, if we want to be top-performing salespeople, we must have all of these regions of our brain operating together. To maintain a good mindset, we must engage the prefrontal cortex in check for logical decision-making, control the amygdala to lessen stress and anxiety, and access the reward centre of our brain for motivation.

When faced with rejection or setbacks, it's natural to become discouraged, but by practicing mindfulness and positive affirmations, you may change your perspective and become more resilient. You may meet your sales goals and prosper in this competitive sector if you have a positive and growth-oriented mindset.

It may appear to be a lot, but with some practice, you will be able to achieve everything you dream of. Good luck!

About the Author

Tim Robertson is a B2B sales performance consultant specialising in behaviour change. He is passionate about sales success in the B2B environment using the latest decision-making and neuroscience methods.

Originally a medical scientist by background, Tim has a career in business and senior management, spanning 30 years during which time he has been a top-performing director and established and run courses on sales, account development, and leadership within the many varied business sectors.

Having recently completed an applied neuroscience course, he is currently undertaking his doctorate in using a novel method of engaging with decision makers faster in initial sales conversations.

Tim has worked across many sectors globally with clients large and small—from two-person start-ups to international conglomerates with household names.

Much of his work is tailoring programs for clients to fit their business models. He has a flexible approachable style.

Email: tim@collaboratesp.com
LinkedIn: https://www.linkedin.com/in/timrobertsoninsight/

CHAPTER EIGHTEEN

SELLING IS SIMPLE; IT JUST FEELS COMPLICATED

By Richard-Løvehjerte Rosendahl
BtoB and BtoC Sales Specialist
Kristiansand, Norway

You must look at facts because they look at you.
—Winston Churchill

Unleashing the power of perception holds the key to unlocking our true potential in the realm of sales. Brace yourself, for it is our beliefs and perceptions that mold our very reality, forging the path of triumph or tribulation. Like a kaleidoscope of possibilities, our beliefs shape our thoughts, ignite our emotions, and propel our actions. In this delicate dance, lies the (lion)heart and soul of sales success.

Small Keys Unlock Large Doors

I was leading a sales training process with a group of communication advisors, and there was a particularly enthusiastic woman among the participants. She had a strong drive to expand her knowledge and improve her skills. Her determination was clear as she sought validation and fresh perspectives to enhance her abilities. With a few minor (mental) adjustments that she implemented, she began to witness remarkable outcomes. In just 12 months, her sales doubled, and astonishingly, she achieved another doubling in the subsequent year.

She already possessed the necessary understanding. All she needed was the confidence to act upon her existing knowledge. However, she faced a challenge—despite the apparent simplicity of selling, she found it to be complicated. She rhetorically asked during a later sales training, "How can something be so simple and yet feel so complex?"

How You View Selling and Life

If you view something as complicated, you are more likely to have a passive approach and focus on avoiding failure. This can lead to a lack of initiative and a tendency to shy away from challenges. However, if you view something as simple and joyful, you may approach it with a lighter attitude and focus on finding solutions. This can lead to a more proactive approach and a willingness to take risks. Essentially, the way we perceive things will influence our attitudes and behaviors towards them, and ultimately affect our level of success.

Most Salespeople Are Far Better Than They Feel

Most people are more aware of their "failures" and flaws than what they do that actually works in sales. This again is because failures and flaws feel strong and painful, both mentally and physically. On top of that, those feelings can breed both fear and shame. The result is that we fear not being enough or being too much. Both situations make us leave our natural selves and start playing a role based on the idea we have about the "perfect" salesperson. Mostly this idea is our own construction, and it works against us. Not for us. We lose ourselves, and then we lose our credibility. We often become the archetype of a salesperson and we become lost in transaction.

On the other hand, when salespeople experience success or do things that work, the feeling is weaker. They may not feel anything or take it for granted because it feels natural. There may be a fleeting sense of lightness or happiness, but it quickly fades, and they continue without noticing it.

Many salespeople feel mediocre and behave accordingly, even though they are brilliant in most situations.

The strength of the feelings associated with failures and flaws is not only painful but also long-lasting. They can linger for hours, days, or even weeks, replaying in our minds and reinforcing their truth. Unfortunately, dwelling on these negative experiences erodes confidence and becomes a self-destructive cycle.

There is no direct connection between how you feel during a sales call and your results. Feeling good in a sales call does not guarantee the desired outcome, and feeling awful does not mean everything is lost. Often, it is the opposite.

My tip is to reflect on what works for you in sales—what you do, how you do it, and when you do it. At the same time, avoid dwelling on your mistakes.

I have spent 25 years of my life as a sales and leadership trainer. In 1998, I was the director of sales for a Scandinavian hotel chain, overseeing 42 hotels and around 50 salespeople. What struck me was the variation in results among the salespeople, despite having similar conditions. I was curious about why some of them were much better than others. It wasn't a matter of certain types of people or differences in experience. The answer was simple: the best salespeople had the right mindsets, working structures, and personal development because they loved their work. They truly enjoyed selling, which gave them the best conditions to evolve and succeed repeatedly. Furthermore, when you genuinely enjoy what you do, it shows to those around you, making you trustworthy and calming. People like being around you.

Selling is often perceived as a complex process that requires unique skills and abilities. Many people believe that it is an art form reserved for a select few. However, this perception couldn't be further from the truth. The perceived complexity of selling stems from the diverse situations it entails, which can lead to friction and frustration for salespeople. Navigating these situations and managing the accompanying emotions can be challenging.

To overcome these challenges, salespeople can benefit from taking a step back and approaching sales situations with a calmer mindset. By adopting a relaxed attitude and utilizing effective strategies, anyone can master the art of selling. It is important to understand that selling is a simple process that can be learned by anyone with the right methods, mindset, and approach.

By recognizing that selling is not as complicated as it may seem, salespeople can navigate the diverse situations they encounter more effectively and achieve better outcomes. With the right mindset and approach, success in selling becomes attainable for everyone.

The Power of Mindset: Your Thinking Shapes Your Reality and Your Actions

As an experiment, I asked Chat.gpt, "What is the right mindset in sales?" Here is the result:

> The right mindset in sales is one that focuses on building long-term relationships with customers, rather than just making a quick sale. **It involves a customer-centric approach where the salesperson prioritizes the needs and wants of the customer above their own.**
>
> In a sales context, a growth mindset is crucial for success. This means being open to learning, embracing challenges, and continuously striving to improve. A salesperson with a growth mindset will see rejection as an opportunity to learn and grow, rather than as a personal failure.
>
> Another important aspect of a right mindset in sales is having a **positive attitude.** Sales can be a challenging and competitive field, and maintaining a positive outlook can help a salesperson stay motivated and resilient in the face of rejection or setbacks. A positive attitude also helps build rapport with customers and creates a welcoming and inviting atmosphere.
>
> Lastly, a right mindset in sales also involves being ethical and honest. **Salespeople who prioritize the customer's needs over their own will focus on providing value and solutions rather than trying to push a product or service that the customer does not need or want.** Honesty and transparency build trust and credibility, which are essential for building long-term relationships with customers.
>
> *Note: the author, bolded certain words, phrases, and sentences in the above content.*

I liked what I read. Maybe it is because it matches 100 percent with my experiences.

Breaking Free from the Traditional Mindset in Sales

In the realm of sales, two primary mindsets exist: the product-centric and the customer-centric. I'd like to explore both.

The Product-Centric Mindset—Push Selling

Push selling, also known as the product-centric mindset, is the prevalent perspective in sales. It revolves around salespeople aiming to maximize the number of customers and the quantity of products or services they sell. The focus is on persuading and convincing customers, with the salesperson primarily concerned with themselves and their offerings.

Salespeople adopting this mindset often appear enthusiastic, employ overly friendly tones, avoid any statements that may be perceived as incorrect, and strive to win customers' favor through flattery and sycophancy.

During customer meetings, the salesperson tends to dominate the conversation, centering it around themselves and their products. Meanwhile, the customer takes on a passive role, primarily listening and occasionally asking questions. The underlying belief is that if the salesperson can make the customer like and trust them, the customer will make a purchase.

Regrettably, a significant number of salespeople, leaders, trainers, and sales books subscribe to this perspective.

But, hey, it works!

Undeniably, the push selling approach can yield considerable short-term success. However, it is highly demanding, antiquated, and often less sustainable. It often leads to customers purchasing things they don't truly need or solutions that don't align with their actual requirements.

However, by shifting from a product-centric to a customer-centric approach, salespeople can experience a transformative change. Instead of being product pushers, they become problem solvers, prioritizing the needs of the customers over the products themselves. Changing this perspective may be more challenging than anticipated, as sales habits and thought patterns are often deeply rooted in product-centricity. It requires a high level of consciousness and presence to effect this change, with the cognitive shift being easier to grasp than the acquisition of new habits and skills.

The Customer-Centric Mindset—Selling Solutions

There are three primary characteristics to consider about customers. The first is that it is the customer's job and responsibility to buy what you sell. The better the solution they choose, the more effectively they can perform in their role. The second is that there may be a significant discrepancy between what customers say they want and what they actually need. The third is that customers are, in many ways, like people in general. Treat them accordingly. Unlike the product-centric mindset, the customer-centric mindset takes into account these three characteristics of customers because it revolves around understanding the customer's needs or problems and providing them with comprehensive solutions through products or services.

Intention—customer-centric salespeople approach their role with the intention to "help to solve." This intention resonates with customers, as they can sense and appreciate it. Remember that your thoughts leak into your interactions.

Empathy—salespeople adopting a customer-centric mindset often possess a strong sense of empathy. They strive to understand the customer's context and situation, going beyond mere facts.

The Core of the Solution Perspective

Salespeople adopting a customer-centric mindset are 100 percent focused on the customers, their situations, and their needs. In this way, the customer-centric mindset operates from a solution perspective. During customer meetings, such salespeople actively listen and ask clear, insightful questions to fully comprehend the customer's requirements. At the core of the solution perspective is an aim to understand your customer's needs or problems (pain) and then to provide complete solutions using your products or services.

The challenge for most salespeople is resisting the temptation to discuss products and solutions prematurely before fully mapping out the customer's needs. Even customers, themselves, may be eager to delve into product discussions before clarifying their actual needs.

Here are some tips to help in this situation:

- Determine the information and facts you need from the customer.
- Make a note of the questions you need to ask to obtain that information.
- Refrain from discussing solutions until you have gathered the necessary information.

From Convincing to Solving

I was conducting a training session for a group of real estate agents and their leaders. One young man in the group was feeling frustrated because he couldn't figure out how to improve his hit rate, the conversion from property inspections to signed contracts. Initially, his success rate was one out of three, or 33 percent. Once he learned about the two mindsets, he completely changed his approach. Instead of focusing on self-presentation and talking about himself, he shifted his focus to genuinely being interested in the customers and asking thoughtful questions. As a result, his interactions with customers improved dramatically. In fact, he achieved a 100 percent hit rate in his next 19 inspections. He realized that he already possessed the necessary knowledge and skills to succeed. It was his mindset and preconceived notions about what made a good inspection that were holding him back. His goal shifted from trying to convince customers to trust him to simply earning their trust through his genuine interest and thoughtful questions. He experienced firsthand that trust is a natural consequence of this approach.

Cracking the Code: Understanding Why Sales Feels Complicated

Sales can often feel like a complex process due to the fear it triggers. It involves situations that remind us of challenging life experiences, where we had to expose ourselves. In sales, we express ourselves through words and actions, making us vulnerable to rejection and exclusion, which are deeply rooted fears in human nature.

Furthermore, negative past experiences, including childhood embarrassments caused by parents, teachers, siblings, or friends can make sales even more challenging. These memories, imprinted in our subconscious, can result in trauma and intensify our emotional responses. As a result, situations that resemble these traumatic experiences, such as approaching people who haven't shown interest, asking for time, or proposing solutions that others may dislike, can evoke similar levels of fear and drama.

Anxious Pushers vs. Calm Solvers: Contrasting Approaches in Sales

In the world of sales, two distinct approaches emerge: anxious pushers and calm solvers. Anxious pushers are primarily driven by their own concerns and strive for flawlessness and frictionless interactions. They believe that if customers like them personally, sales will naturally follow suit. Their ultimate fear is rejection, as a "no" feels deeply personal to them.

On the other hand, calm solvers embody a more composed and pragmatic mindset. They approach various situations with enthusiasm but without excessive worry. They understand that their success hinges on identifying the right customers, engaging with them, and effectively addressing their needs. When faced with a customer's rejection, they recognize that it is often a result of the situation or the proposed solution rather than a reflection on themselves as salespeople.

The following sales-related situations can evoke various fears and anxieties, such as rejection, failure, inadequacy, embarrassment, being perceived as pushy, losing control, and more:

- Approaching people who haven't expressed interest (e.g., cold-calling)
- Requesting time from others (e.g., scheduling a meeting)
- Contacting busy individuals (e.g., follow-up calls)
- Presenting proposals or pitches that others may not like
- Meeting experts in their field as a potential client
- Engaging with people of higher status or position
- Persistent follow-up when met with non-responsiveness

It is critical that you, as a salesperson, recognize which (if any) common sales situations trigger you emotionally so that you can manage yourself and better stay in calm-solver mode.

To become a skilled salesperson, it is crucial to learn how to manage the emotions that can arise in sales situations. Instead of fighting against challenging emotions, it is beneficial to accept and reflect upon them. Consider the situations that you find most demanding, analyze your thoughts and feelings before, during, and after those events, and examine your expectations in those circumstances.

Focusing on the outcome of each situation is essential when reflecting. Evaluate whether you achieved your goal or not, and identify the actions that led to the result. Acknowledge the positive aspects of your efforts and determine areas for improvement.

It's important to recognize that excitement and fear can feel similar in the body. Many times, what we perceive as fear is actually excitement. Being aware of this difference is crucial, as our behavior can vary significantly depending on whether we feel excited or afraid/anxious.

Unlocking Mental Resilience: Embrace Growth and Excel Through Cold Calling

Managing emotions is a skill that requires practice and a method. Cold calling offers an opportunity to develop essential sales skills, including leading conversations, asking clear questions, managing objections and fear, listening attentively, providing clear information, and identifying the right customers.

Despite its reputation, cold calling can be transformed into a skill-building exercise by following a few simple steps:

- Create a list of 50 to 100 prospects on paper.
- Minimize distractions, such as email.
- Develop a method for cold calling.
- Dedicate 60 minutes of uninterrupted calling.
- Schedule your calls between 9.00 and 10.00 am, five days a week, for four weeks.

After just 20 hours of practice—one hour a day for four weeks—you will emerge as a new salesperson with improved skills and enhanced confidence. Embrace the opportunity to overcome fear and unlock your potential.

Resilience Unleashed: Empowering Tips for Success in Sales and Personal Growth

- Manage your emotions to effectively navigate situations.
- Cultivate inner peace and maintain a calm demeanor.
- Identify your successful actions and replicate them.
- Recognize your true capabilities, which often surpass your self-perception.
- Reflect on past sales successes and embrace further growth.

- Look inward for the keys to solving challenges.
- Understand and manage your emotions' impact on your well-being.
- Explore the thoughts that give rise to your emotions.
- Take necessary actions and communicate effectively despite your emotions.
- Embrace discomfort outside your comfort zone as the path to growth.
- Learn from failures and quickly bounce back without taking it personally.
- Dare to seek knowledge and expand your understanding.
- Be courageous in leading others.
- Prioritize self-care and well-being.
- Embrace and enjoy the journey of personal and professional growth.
- And finally: be aware of your self-talk. Talk to yourself like you would talk to your best friend.

About the Author

Richard-Løvehjerte Rosendahl is a low profiled seasoned sales specialist, leadership trainer, public speaker, and commercial development advisor with a career spanning 25 years. His expertise lies in both BtoB and BtoC sectors, with a special focus on knowledge-intensive industries such as advisory services, law, and offshore operations. In the BtoC realm, he excels in cultivating sales cultures within chains, working from the top-down, from CEOs to frontline employees.

Richard's approach to sales and leadership is rooted in the belief that success is determined by how you perceive your role, your intentions in performing it, and the value you create for others. His methodologies are not just theories; they are best practices honed over decades of experience.

As a sought-after public speaker, Richard inspires audiences with his insights into sales and leadership. His advisory work with leader groups in commercial development has led to transformative changes in businesses across various sectors.

His work is characterized by a deep understanding of the human element in sales and leadership. He believes in empowering individuals to see beyond the transaction, to understand the profound impact they can have on others, and to use this understanding to drive success.

Whether he's working with advisors, lawyers, frontline staff, or speaking to an audience, Richard's mission remains the same: to transform the way people think about sales and leadership, and to help them unlock their true potential.

Email: richard@in2win.no
Website: www.in2win.no
LinkedIn: linkedin.com/in/richardjacobsen

CHAPTER NINTEEN
THE FOUR KEYS

By Adam P. Smith
Sales Coach & Keynote Speaker
Denver, Colorado

In order to finish first, you have to first finish.
—Alan Pflueger

Having a proper mindset for a successful sales career, business, or job is one of the most important pieces of the sales success puzzle. We all know that sales, true sales—and not the manipulation some people call "sales"—is not for everyone. It takes a lot to be in sales, and even more to be good at sales. And good salespeople are the ones that are in it to solve problems and help people, not to manipulate a potential buyer. Long gone are the days of the good salespeople being able to "sell ice to Eskimos." Now, good salespeople find pain points and then solutions. That's a major sales mindset shift in recent decades and hopefully you've made that shift too.

We all talk about, read about, and hear about things like attitude and effort, all the time. I remember that general message as far back as the *kitten hanging from a rope* poster in my second-grade classroom. "Hang in there," right? Attitude and effort are certainly very important, but without the proper tools and techniques to execute on, they go to waste. You might have the best attitude, want to act at an amazing level of effort, and have all the right pieces in place with what you're selling, your team, your process, and your logistics, but it may be all for naught.

From the days of Zig Ziglar to Tony Robbins and through to today, we've all been spoken to, coached on, or have read about the "why." That one has also been around forever in the realm of the sales mindset. You've got to have your "why". You have to identify what your "why" is and why it's important. Now, I don't want to belittle or demean how important these things are, but with all the sales training history, with all the years and articles and speakers and books and videos, we're rarely given the details. Nobody ever gives us the nuts and bolts. Those tactical and transactional pieces to build a successful sales machine are locked up tight. The keys for how to execute are being withheld and we need them in order to execute, so we can accomplish great things with all that attitude and effort and, of course, the "why." We simply aren't given enough content on what to do and how to do it to honor that sales mindset we should be exercising and executing every day. That is what I hope this chapter will do for you, at least to some degree.

There are four keys to a successful sales strategy, sales business, or sales career. And they all intertwine to create a successful sales mindset that enables full and proper use of your attitude and effort. When all are executed together, we no longer waste those internal, self-built assets, and we capitalize on them properly. They work together to unlock a door that leads to successful lead generation, closing more deals, retaining more clients and customers while having them all refer new ones, and building up sales and operations teams to handle those leads and clients and business.

No one key is more important than another and all must be executed and respected equally. If you can do that, the potential for your sales, your business, your income, and your legacy are virtually limitless. So, let's rattle this proverbial keyring and talk about the keys.

Key One—Constancy

The first key is constancy. You must be constant in everything you do. From getting up with your alarm clock at the same time every day to reading to your children every night. You must be constant. This must include everything you do in your business, as well. When you execute a marketing idea, business plan, or lead generation tactic, you must be constant with it. Anything less and you will get the exact results to match your efforts.

You want to have constant leads? Then you must be constant in your lead generation. You want to have constant sales success? Then you must have constant sales execution. You want to have constant growth in your business? Then you must be constant in building and managing your teams. We often hear about the roller coaster, the ups and downs, that salespeople are all plagued with in their leads, their business, and their income. This is one of the primary reasons that happens. They are not constant about the things they should be doing, and the results are a perfect reflection. The bottom line is that if your sales mindset and your sales work is up and down with no constancy, so are your results.

A great example of this came from a former coaching client. He was a young guy, a new real estate agent and new to our program. But he was eager to begin his sales career and was willing to take on all kinds of new lead gen tactics. At one point, he told me he wanted to start doing door knocking. For those of you not in real estate, the tactic is essentially picking out neighborhoods you want to do business in and knocking on the doors of the current homeowners or tenants there. You introduce yourself, hopefully chat them up, add them to your audience and database, and maybe even find someone who is looking to sell their home, buy a home, or maybe even both in the not-too-distant future. When executed well, this is a great audience-building technique that could result in new clients, leads, and advocates for the long term, and even has some potential for closed deals in the near future. Everyone either owns real estate, wants to, or knows someone who does, so this is a common lead generation tactic in real estate. And if done constantly, a good one.

I told him this wasn't a tactic I would employ, as I think the time spend for the ROI is a little off and that I would rather spend that time talking to larger audiences, like I do on social media, or with good video work, but he wanted to try. Now, I will never judge someone for how they do their lead generation work, but I surely will if they don't do it, and do it constantly. He told me he was going to do four hours every weekend. That's a lot of shoe leather, especially considering the dichotomy that higher-end neighborhoods with potentially higher commissions have homes likely much farther apart while others may have a greater population density and more potential contacts. Nonetheless, I told him he should go for it. And after a month he came back to me and told me that it didn't work. He did four hours, once a week, for a month. That's a total of roughly sixteen hours. Pretty much a single workday in the life of a new real estate agent, or any salesperson, if they want to succeed. Tell me it sucked. Tell me you hated doing it. But don't tell me it didn't work.

If you did that for four hours every weekend for a year, it would undoubtedly work. But he wasn't constant with that activity.

Key Two—Consistency

The second key is consistency. You must be just as consistent in everything you do as you are constant. This also applies to everything in your life, not just the sales activities and your sales mindset. And this one is different. And maybe even a little easier. Being consistent doesn't mean you have to do a thousand things in your personal and business life every day until you're dead. It means you must have a plan. A constant plan. And you must execute on it consistently. Maybe your bandwidth only has room for working out once a week. That's fine. But you must do it every week, consistently. Perhaps your lead gen plan includes doing a live video on one social media platform or another twice a month. That's great. If you actually do it two times every month. Whatever it is, it must be consistent.

We work with our clients incessantly on video. And video campaigns are a great sales technique and tactic, but it only works if done consistently. This is true for both the videos for the clients you have, as that is part of securing repeat and referral business, and for the clients you want. And without fail, many people create video plans on both fronts, come up with the content, outline the frequency, get a grip on recording, editing, and distribution, and then fail to be consistent. I remember a past client, a bartender in a previous life, who thought it would be a good idea to do a video campaign, once a week, teaching his audiences how to make a different cocktail with each episode. And he was right. It was a good idea. And it got a ton of traction. But then he became complacent and inconsistent with it and people noticed. People in his audiences began to reach out to him and ask why he'd stopped doing them. Or at least doing them on the regular. If your audiences, the people you want to buy from you, notice your inconsistency, that's a problem. You must be consistent.

Key Three—Authenticity

The third key is authenticity. Being authentic in your sales mindset is going to be one of the greatest tools you can develop and use to further your sales career.

You know why people still look at salespeople like the used car salesmen of yesteryear? Why is it still such a horrible cliché to be in sales? Because so many of us now, and so many of us then, have never been authentic. Those people didn't get into sales for the right reasons. They don't believe in the product they are selling. They are more interested in the deal than they are in the client. They are salespeople, in the most degrading and derogatory sense of the word, for all those reasons.

But it doesn't have to be that way. We know that good sales work, and good salespeople are all about finding pain points and then solving those problems. And being authentic in wanting to help people and to solve their problems is crucial. I believe it was Zig Ziglar who said that all you have to do is help as many people as you can get what they want, and you're going to get what you want. And he was right. I have even gone so far as to print a large label that reads: "WE'RE HERE TO HELP PEOPLE!" and have it taped to the bottom of my computer monitor, so I never forget that part of my "why."

One of the greatest skills a salesperson can have that really honors the authenticity key is the ability to listen. Now, this is a tough one for many of us. Salespeople love to talk. We really do. It's one of the things that makes salespeople so good at sales. But odds are good that we talk way too much, and we don't listen nearly enough. You know it's true. If you can shut up and listen, people are going to talk to you. People love to talk about themselves, whether they're in sales or not. And the more you listen, the more they will talk. And that talk will eventually turn to those pain points, which is when you and your cape step in, solve problems, be the hero, and have authentic success in sales.

Key Four—Transparency

The final key is transparency. This one escapes a lot of people because they don't think their audiences want to know who they really are or what really goes on in their lives. Or even worse, they're hiding something and can't be transparent about what they're selling or why they're selling it. Well, the former ones, they're wrong. That's all people want to know these days. They want to know who you are much more than they want to know what you do. Or what you sell, in this case. If you're already using the other keys, they already know what you do. They already know what you sell. If they don't, or if anyone in your audiences doesn't know what you do or what you sell by this point, we need to go back to Marketing 101.

The fact is, we've all been someone's target audience since birth. And we're sick of it. We have all had enough marketing shoved down our throats, from television and radio and print media to the global network and social media and on and on, to last us a lifetime. But it keeps coming. And it always will. Yet, we rarely see the day-to-day trials and tribulations of Jim Walton. We don't know that Steve Ballmer's granddaughter had a tonsillectomy. I'm not sure what Warren Buffet cooked for dinner. And that makes them surreal. They are untouchables, as it were. And not only do their lives mean little to me and my "why," but I wouldn't buy anything they were directly selling to me because of it. There's no human transparency with Wal-Mart or Microsoft or Berkshire Hathaway. And today, people want to know who you are, not what you do.

People want to buy from people they know, like, and trust. You've heard that one before too, but it's true. And since we've all been that target audience from birth, especially people buying whatever it is you're selling today, they care much more about who you are. What kind of person you are. What you have in common with them. What you believe in. What you stand for and support. In essence, they want to know that you're not just a sales machine. For example, if you're the person who doesn't let the public, or especially your potential clients and customers, see your social media because you don't want them to see what you do in your personal life, that's a problem. You must be transparent. Or you might just need to stop doing whatever it is you're doing that you wouldn't want them to see.

The best part is that you can deliver that transparency to a broad audience with the tools we have today like social media and video. And that is an edge on building that "know, like, and trust." They say you need something between eight and a gazillion interactions with someone for enough traction that they do know, like, and trust you enough to buy from you or work with you. The tools available to us today to be authentic and transparent, for virtually no cost, could easily cut that number in half. By doing good, authentic, and transparent social media or video work, you're giving people some serious insight as to who you are and not just what you do. My audiences know how I speak. They know my tone, my inflection, my sense of humor. And they know my wardrobe and what my office looks like and what my home office looks like and even the inside of my car. They know my wife and my children and my pets. I am a real, authentic, transparent person, to the masses, because of those tools.

The result of this is astounding. It actually took me a long time to adjust to the paparazzi-esque byproduct of these keys. But a great example was an episode that occurred in the Denver International Airport. I was traveling to a conference in Atlanta, standing in line at security, waiting for my bag to come through the X-ray machine, and I was not my usual self. At least not the person my audiences typically know. I was wearing long pants and a sport coat, and I'm usually a shorts and t-shirt kind of guy. And I was wearing a face mask because that was the style of the time. Different wardrobe, my face covered, not my usual monologuing and the woman behind me asked, "Aren't you Adam Smith?" I admitted to it, and she proceeded to talk to me like she knew me. And she did know me. She had been consuming what could have been years and years of constant, consistent, authentic, and transparent content from me and the result was just that. She knew me. And she knew me, liked me, and trusted me enough to chat with me all the way down to the train and out to the concourse, and she even shared some authentic and personal things with me along the way. Even some of her pain points. And I had never met her. What an amazing opportunity for me to solve problems, make sales, help people, and get paid, all because of the keys.

Now when people talk to me like they know me or interact with me that way in the digital world, despite never having actually met them, I understand what led me here. I can see that the work over many years led me to understand sales is a career and not just a job, a marathon, not a sprint, and this paid dividends. Having spent so long with a sales mindset built on constancy, consistency, authenticity, and transparency and implementing that into all my techniques and tactics led to this point. My sales mindset was built on those four keys and is implemented in everything I do in my business. And all this led to a fulfilling and successful sales career, a solid work-life balance, and an ideal sales mindset. Hopefully it will for you too.

About the Author

Adam P. Smith is one of the country's leading minds in lead generation and team structure. His broad mortgage origination and broker-owner experience and teaching others in similar industries on the subject led him to becoming an authority on lead generation, client retention, repeat and referral sales prospecting, zero cost marketing, and building sales and operations teams. In 2019, he published *Just the Tips*, a result of all the tips he has used and taught on the subject, structured in a fun and quirky way, to help other salespeople understand what has brought Adam his success as a mortgage originator, a teacher and coach, and as an author.

Adam is a fourth generation Denver native and grew up in the south Denver and surrounding suburban areas. He is married to long-time Colorado resident, Elizabeth, and has three children, Lisa, Alex, and Asher. Adam is an avid sports fan and is a season ticket holder for the Denver Broncos, Colorado Avalanche, Denver Nuggets, and the University of Denver Pioneers.

Email: justthetipscoaching@gmail.com
Website: www.justthetipscoaching.com

CHAPTER TWENTY
SUCCESS IN PLAIN SIGHT

By David Snyder
Speaker, Trainer, Prosperity Mindset Coach
Windsor, Ontario, Canada

When you change the way you look at things, the things you look at change.
—Wayne Dyer

Take a moment and let those words sink in. Read that quote again if you have to. What does it mean to you?

This quote has been one of the most influential truths that I've applied throughout my life. It has been a constant reminder for me to shift my mindset in situations that have left me feeling confused, discouraged, lost, and defeated. Have those thoughts ever crept into your mind when reflecting on sales or performance? Have you questioned whether you're on the right path? Have you asked yourself, "Am I really cut out to be in sales?"

I can guarantee you that at some point in your career, you've had at least one of these thoughts and to be honest, you've likely experienced them multiple times. A career in sales can be daunting and emotionally exhausting because we're dealing with the human experience and directly reflecting our wins and losses back on our ourselves. The rejection, stress, feelings of inadequacy, and persistent pressure to consistently perform can be relentless. It can break down the human spirit, leading us to burnout and perpetual failure—from both an internal and external perspective.

I'm sure you're wondering where I'm going with this and why anyone would even want to be in sales after reading the above. The answer to that question is because with the right mindset sales can be an incredibly rewarding and enjoyable career.

In this chapter I'll share with you five principles that have helped me to cultivate a prosperous mindset and how I change the way I look at things every single day.

Don't Lose the Lesson

Some of life's greatest lessons are the ones that you don't realize you've learned until years, even decades later. It's only when someone asks you, "Where did you learn that?" Then, you take a moment to reflect on the source and realize the teachings that were hidden within an experience.

I was born into a multi-generational entrepreneurial family where business and sales were interwoven into the fabric of our everyday lives. Every moment that my older brother and I weren't in school or playing sports, we were in our father's store. This allowed me to deepen my understanding of the human experience from a very early age. I would sit at the back of the store and watch people for hours, listening to the sales team serve our customers, observing my dad with fascination as he managed and taught his employees, and witnessing the community who would return over and over again.

Looking back on these memories, I realize that most of the things I now teach in sales were never taught to me; they were caught. School did a great job teaching me what to think, but never was I sat down and told how I needed to think. That was a bug I caught over 40 years ago without even knowing, as I sat on that stool behind the cash register in awe of the human experience happening in front of me.

Don't lose the lesson. Even when you think you aren't learning, you are. You're absorbing the world around you in ways you may not even realize. Change the way you view the interactions you have each day and don't take any of them for granted, even if the conversations appear to be insignificant. Take that extra moment in the meeting to get to know your customer. They may just share with you the key to their business without even realizing it.

Don't Sell. Help People to Buy

Traditionally, a salesperson has not been a career of choice with most people having often fallen into it by default. Perhaps your educational path came to an end and you didn't know where to turn for the next season of your life; or you didn't finish post-secondary education and needed a job; or someone suggested sales because you have the "gift of the gab." (Check off all of the above for me.)

Hollywood has done a great job of portraying salespeople in a negative light (insert the used car salesman, managers screaming for numbers, and a life that is so stressful drugs and alcohol are a needed crutch). As a result of this characterization, when someone mentions sales, it's only natural for our thoughts to immediately drift to this Hollywood sales persona illustrated in our minds. Our mindset becomes hijacked by this unfavorable depiction of sales, where the salesperson is *never* the hero. Inevitably we may begin to adopt the habits and actions of some of those pushy, slimy characters and spend our days pitching a product or service to anyone who will listen, praying that we can just sell something to someone.

In my experience, salespeople who have this mindset have a short shelf life, either with their employer or the industry in general. They don't connect with their customers, they don't sell on value, they pitch products that their customers may not even need, and at the end of the day, their focus is meeting their own target and not helping their customer meet theirs.

By changing how you approach and engage with your customers, you can become an advisor, not just for this transaction but also for the next phase of your customer's business.

The peak performing salesperson approaches each customer with the intention of either finding a solution to a problem they can help the customer fix or improving upon what the customer's business is currently doing. Their mission in this role isn't to sell, but to help their customers buy.

Like Riding a Bike

If you've ever learned how to ride a bike, you've probably already gone through the exercise of finding your "why" without even knowing it.

The big moment arrived when you were finally ready to take off the training wheels. Off they came and you were on your way with someone holding on to the back of the seat until you (shockingly) realized that they were no longer holding on. Total panic ensued and down you went. After a few tears and a comforting hug, what was the first thing you wanted to do? You likely wanted to get back up on the bike and try again. The "why" you needed to learn to ride the bike was more powerful than the pain you experienced from falling off.

What is your "why" in sales?

The world of sales is fast paced and competitive. Every month a new game begins and the score sets back to 0–0. For some this can be a relief, for others it's the moment they dread. You've descended back down the mountain and have to make the trek up all over again. You may try to focus on one large deal and push off parts of the job that you hate, like prospecting. This vicious cycle can take its toll on salespeople who are not practicing the right mindset. The reality is that this becomes a "pay now or pay later" situation. Either you pay the price that is the pain and discomfort of the activity you dislike or you pay later when the month closes and you haven't hit your target.

Peak performers don't allow themselves to push off the tedious daily fundamentals, even if they don't like doing them. They've created resiliency by finding their "why" and can easily get up in the morning, hit the pavement, and tackle their day, week, month, quarter, etc. They've found leverage on themselves by believing that the temporary pain from doing the mundane tasks pales in comparison with their reason for doing the work.

Every "why" is different. It may be for the achievement, to build a better life, to prove the naysayers wrong, or simply to help others. It really doesn't matter what your "why" is as long as it's enough to inspire you to overcome the instant gratification of pushing off the activity you dislike.

You may have decided your "why" at the beginning of your sales career and don't think you need to revisit it. I challenge you to change your thinking here. As your career (and life) progresses, so will your "why." Take the time to do an honest introspection. Is your "why" today the same as it was when you started?

Find the best way to remind yourself daily of "why" you do what you do, and those tedious fundamentals will eventually become easier, setting you up for future success.

Don't Play "Prevent Defence"

Many parallels can be found in sports and sales and I, for one, love to make them. One that immediately comes to mind when discussing mindset is football's "prevent defence."

When a football team is holding on to a small lead with time winding down in the fourth quarter, they'll switch their style of play to uber-conservative, staying back and protecting their end zone. This may allow the opposing team to gain a few short plays, but the goal is to run the clock before the opposing team can score. Although the intention of the prevent defence is to play it safe and win the game, it can often backfire as the team throws out the strategy that made them dominate 98 percent of the game, allowing the opposing team to gain momentum and potentially score.

This same mindset can be what is holding you back in your sales career. Maybe you sit back and do the bare minimum at the end of the month, running out the clock. It's easy to fall into this trap of playing "not to lose," but eventually it will provoke a salesperson to focus on anything and everything that can go wrong. This can develop into fear that leads to stress, anxiety, and a loss of confidence. Change the way you look at this.

Peak performers play to win, every day, every month. Regardless of where they are in relation to their monthly sales targets, they don't settle or slow down when they're in the lead. They approach each day with the same intensity, passion, game plan, and sense of urgency.

Limiting Beliefs

One of the most effective changes you can make to your sales mindset is how you view and talk to yourself.

Ask a hundred salespeople what is preventing them from taking their sales careers to the next level, and you may very well get a hundred different answers. However, chances are that not one of them will say that their biggest challenge is themselves.

The tendency is to look outward, trying to place blame on something or someone else, and in this practice, we miss the opportunity for growth. Interestingly enough, having a negative or limiting belief in yourself is most often the culprit for the challenges we experience, and it's one of those things that you'll only notice when you're looking for it.

This negative self-talk can take many forms. Saying things such as, "I'll never make President's Club," "I'm terrible at making cold-calls," or "I can't hit my target because my territory sucks," will become self-fulfilling prophecies.

Change the way you speak to yourself.

Peak performers understand that junk in is junk out. Keep feeding your mind negative self-talk (junk in), and you'll consistently put up sub-par performances (junk out). To achieve at the peak level, you must audit yourself regularly as the seeds of doubt can be found wherever there is a crack.

Here's a blueprint that works in my own practice:

1. Extract Your Thoughts

Find a quiet place and list out any negative thoughts that you have about your job, company, product/service, and most importantly, yourself. Don't overthink. Just start writing whatever comes to mind. The more you write, the more thoughts will rise to the surface.

2. Evaluate Your Thoughts

Go through each of these points one by one, and look at them objectively. How would you evaluate a friend or colleague who is doing the same exercise? Ask yourself, "Why do I feel this way?" and use the five-why method. When you can provide an objective answer, ask yourself, "Why?" again. Do this five times. Often the true root cause of the negative self-talk takes a bit of time to uncover.

3. Flip the Narrative

Once you understand the root cause of the negative self-talk, take the questions and transform them into positive and inspiring thoughts. For example, thoughts like "I suck at cold calling" can flip to "I have an opportunity to get better at cold calling."

4. Activate New Thoughts

Take these new positive statements and set a new standard for yourself. Create a plan that will help you achieve small wins that you'll take every day to maintain the new standard.

If you ever watch a Formula 1 race, you'll observe the entire racing team constantly analyzing data to improve lap times. However, instead of looking at the entire lap time and simply telling the driver they have to go faster, the team breaks the race track down into small intervals. They analyse the times through each of these intervals and find ways that the driver can tweak their approach to each turn or straightaway to chisel down a fraction of a second. Doing the same exercise for each interval will naturally give a better overall result: a faster lap time.

Change the way you look at improvement in your process.

You don't need to improve the speed of the lap right away. Work on small attainable actions that will help you shave off those precious seconds. As the saying goes, don't let perfection get in the way of progress.

5. Give Yourself Grace

It's not a question of if you have setbacks, it's when you'll have setbacks. These are all part of the process. There will be days when your old negative self-talk will creep in because of something outside of your control. Give yourself permission and time to feel upset, but move on from it. Remind yourself of those negative self-talk points that you flipped into positive statements and beliefs.

Peak performers still deal with negative self-talk, but the key for their success is that they don't allow themselves too much time to bathe in it.

6. An Empowering Inner Circle

As much as positivity can be caught versus being taught, so can negativity. Your environment and the people you surround yourself with could very well be responsible for you catching some of your negative self-talk without you even realizing it.

As you raise your game and take your career to the next level, your inner circle's minds will go to self-preservation as your success may leave them anxious that you're going to leave them behind. This can be seen in the "crab mentality" where crabs will sabotage the escape of another crab from a bucket by pulling them down before they reach the top.

There's also a very popular theory to support this idea called tall poppy syndrome. It refers to the actual cutting of poppies. In an agricultural sense, it's believed that poppies should grow at the same rate, resulting in equal height for all flowers. When one poppy grows taller than the other flowers, it's cut down in order to maintain an esthetically even field when viewed from a distance. In a business context, the term started in Australia and New Zealand, referring to a situation when an individual's success makes others resentful, bringing on an onslaught of criticism or personal attacks. Like the literal flower, when a person grows too high, too fast, they get cut down for standing out.

Change the way you look at your peers and friends.

Peak performers evaluate their inner circle throughout their journey. They surround themselves with like-minded people that inspire them and help them grow. They know that their closest inner circle is allowed to evolve, like them. They learn to identify those who unintentionally try to pull them back down and prevent their comments and actions from discouraging them.

Take time to sit down and list out the five people that you spend the most time with. If any of these people are feeding the negative self-talk, understand that you will have to adjust how you interact with them. You don't necessarily have to cut them out of your life entirely (most of these people may even be family), but you can be aware of what is happening and you can begin to deflect their negative energy to not let it affect your mindset.

Change Is Constant

Imagine the you from five years ago. Do you still have the same outlook on life? Feel the same about your career? Would the you from today listen to the you from five years ago?

If we're really being honest with ourselves, the answer to all of these questions is no. We're all different people from who we were five years ago, five months ago, five weeks ago, you get the drift. Change is constant. The principles I've highlighted in this chapter are not a one-time exercise to focus on, they are a lifestyle.

Peak performers understand this, knowing that the key to their success is their ability to embrace a growth mindset and keep learning. To see themselves as sherpas, taking the customer's baggage on their backs, supporting them throughout the journey, and leading them up the rocky terrain as they approach the purchase pinnacle. They fully live inside of their "why" and are consistently breaking the pattern of negative self-talk.

I challenge you to continue to change the way you look at things. Reevaluate who you are and what you're doing, and the world around you will respond. It is my utmost belief that when our energy is shifted towards a prosperity mindset, peak performance in sales, business, and life is right around the corner.

About the Author

David Snyder is founder and president of PONO Learning, a sales training company that was built on the principle that "complexity is the enemy of execution," creating prosperous learning experiences for sales and service people.

Over the past 30 years David has worked in a variety of industries and has been affiliated with some of the top sales organizations in North America. He's led two national wireless start-ups, founded a golf distribution company, and co-owned both an auto design company as well as an international consulting and sales training firm.

David is an experienced speaker, sales trainer, mindset coach, and certified Answer Intelligence (AQ)™ partner. His mission in life is to be a catalyst for anyone in sales to develop new ways of thinking in order to see that sales isn't that complicated.

Email: dsnyder@ponolearning.com
Website: www.ponolearning.com
Social Media: @ponolearning
@thesalesinterpreter

CHAPTER TWENTY-ONE
THE ULTIMATE SALES PRESENTATION

By Garry Terhune
Sales Presentations Coach
Fairport, New York

Anybody who succeeds is helping people. The secret to success is find a need and fill it; find a hurt and heal it; find a problem and solve it.
—Robert H. Schuller

The sales presentation is the championship of the sales process. This is where sales are ultimately won or lost. There is no second place.

Are you delivering exceptional sales presentations ... every time?

If not, you are losing business that could have been won. Don't let less than stellar sales presentations sabotage all the time and effort spent in the earlier stages of the sales process.

In this chapter we will focus on three key elements of delivering exceptional sales presentations. Each element has three parts:

1. The Ultimate Sales Presentation℠: the three steps of discover—design—deliver
2. The motivators: the three reasons why people buy.
3. Aspects of character: the three qualities that compel people to do business with you

As you will see, these three elements will help you to establish and maintain a winning mindset that will increase the likelihood of winning the sale. What is that winning mindset? Let's see.

A Motivator-Focused Mindset

It's not initially about how great your product, service, experience, or company is. It begins with a motivator-focused mindset. This means understanding what is motivating a prospective customer to take action or understanding what would motivate a prospective customer to take action. Understanding their motivators will best position you to design and deliver a presentation that will truly resonate with them. Understanding their motivators will best position the prospective customer to benefit from your offering.

Let's start with element one.

1: The Ultimate Sales Presentation^{sm}

The Ultimate Sales Presentation^{sm} is a methodology designed based on my 40-plus years in sales, delivering sales presentations, conducting sales presentations training, and performing sales presentations coaching.

The Ultimate Sales Presentation^{sm} is—

a) A well-earned opportunity for you to introduce your offering, ask for the sale, and best position yourself to receive a "yes"

b) An opportunity for a prospective customer (soon-to-be customer) to set in motion the acquisition of a product, service, or experience that will satisfy their motivator(s) and affect their desired state

The three steps of The Ultimate Sales Presentation^{sm} include the following:

Step 1—DISCOVER
Discover Why People Say Yes

It all begins by understanding motivators. It is in the discover phase where you'll learn about their primary motivator, perhaps a secondary motivator, and at times even a tertiary motivator. Motivators are behind why people desire what they desire, do what they do, buy what they buy, and buy into what they buy into. People buy feelings. When your particular expertise can address these motivators and the feelings associated with satisfying the motivators, you can be invaluable to people. Begin where your prospective customer currently is. The discover step will position you to address their most urgent need(s). What you learn in discover will essentially design your sales presentation. What you learn in discover will position you to deliver a sales presentation that will truly resonate with the prospective customer.

Step 2—DESIGN
Design the Ultimate Sales Presentation^{sm}
for Maximum Positive Impact

Your presentation will be based on a thorough understanding of your prospective customer's motivators and associated feelings learned in the discover step. The design step is about crafting a compelling and convincing sales presentation that is focused and meaningful to your prospective customer's specific situation. The design step includes often quoting the prospective customer.

Step 3—DELIVER
Deliver the Ultimate Sales Presentation^{sm}
with Maximum Positive Impact

You're on! This is your opportunity. Perhaps your only opportunity. Here is where you take what you've learned in discover and crafted in design, and you bring it to life in this deliver step. What your audience sees and hears when you're presenting is crucial! How you come across can make or break your presentation. Don't sabotage your value with a lacking presentation of your offering. Look and sound like you mean business. Come across with energy, conviction, and clarity. The deliver step positions you to achieve your desired outcome (receiving a yes) by showing, telling, and asking your audience how you can help them achieve their desired outcome. The deliver step includes often quoting the prospective customer.

Scenarios and Settings
Rest assured the Ultimate Sales Presentation^{sm} methodology works. It works for a sales cycle of any length. All three steps of the Ultimate Sales Presentation^{sm}

can be encapsulated into one single conversation in one meeting or any number of conversations and meetings over any period of time.

It works in any setting. For example—

- Seated across a desk
- Seated around a conference room table
- Seated around a kitchen table
- Standing or seated in a boardroom
- Standing in an amphitheater
- Standing in a conference room
- In an office
- Virtually

It works whether the setting is formal or informal. The Ultimate Sales Presentation℠ works if you informally design the sales presentation on the fly with a pencil and paper based on the notes you're taking when communicating with the potential customer. It also works if you have a design expert helping you to craft a more formal sales presentation based on what you've learned in discover that will be delivered in a formal setting.

For any scenario and setting, you must design and deliver a crystal-clear sales presentation because confused minds say no.

Let's now focus on chapter element two to learn why people buy.

2: MotivatorsThe three motivators behind why people buy products, services, or experiences are—

1. To relieve existing pain
2. To avoid potential pain
3. To achieve gain

Let's look at the first two—to relieve existing pain and to avoid potential pain.

Existing or potential pain is anything negative a person desires to remove or avoid: problems, challenges, obstacles, roadblocks, difficulties, complications, issues, setbacks, loss, physical pain, emotional pain, frustration, danger, fear, etc.

When someone is experiencing existing pain, it's hard to focus on anything else. People will do almost anything to relieve the pain. Motivation to relieve existing pain is typically high depending on the seriousness and level of the pain. Pain relief has a level of urgency. The more painful, the more urgent to relieve. To uncover and understand their level of urgency, knowing where they currently are is critical.

Regarding avoiding potential pain, people might not even be aware of lurking potential pain. Be invaluable by alerting them. Be even more invaluable by helping them to avoid the potential pain. If your offering is positioned to do so, be sure to present how your offering will help them do so. They will be grateful you helped them to avoid pain they didn't see coming.

The third motivator behind why people buy products, services, and experiences is to achieve gain. Gain meaning anything positive a person desires to achieve or attain. This includes aspirations, dreams, goals, success, progress, prosperity, security, advancement, growth, financial gain, financial security, physical well-being, emotional well-being, improvement, safety remedy, peace, happiness, etc.

How hot is their desire? Again, there are various levels of urgency. Uncover and understand their level of urgency.

You will learn of their motivators during the discover step of the Ultimate Sales Presentation^{SM} process.

How to Uncover and Understand People's Motivators

To uncover their motivators, ask strategic questions. In other words, position when and where you use the following various types of questions at your disposal.

Open questions—as all seasoned salespeople know, open questions typically begin with the words—what, how, or why. Open questions elicit richer information. Drill down on their answers to uncover more specifics by using prompts.

Prompts—prompts are like questions without question marks. "Tell me more." "Please elaborate." Prompts also elicit richer information and provide an alternative to an open question.

Echoes—Repeat back to them a key word they've spoken with inflection in your voice. Sound like you're asking a one-word question. "Troubling?" "Crucial?" People tend to respond to an echo and provide more information.

Conditional—I call conditional questions dreaming questions. They begin with "If … ?" or "What if … ?" They invite people to envision the future without pressure.

Closed—use closed questions to ask for details and specifics: who, how many, when, etc. Be aware of getting in the habit of using too many closed questions. You'll find yourself working much too hard trying to come up with questions.

Listening is also critical. I've had the pleasure of representing a key client for many years as a contract coach. They contract me out to coach their clients in one-on-one coaching interactions. In those one-on-one coaching situations, the potential coachee interviews or auditions several potential coaches to see who they'd like to work with. I've had the good fortune to win a large percentage of those opportunities.

Once, when speaking with a principal of my client, they said to me, "It seems like every time you talk to someone, you win the business." I thought about this for a moment and then replied, "Actually, every time I listen to someone, I win the business."

People are craving to be heard. People appreciate it when someone truly listens. Be a world-class listener. How? Here are some recommendations:

Validated hearing—once you ask strategic questions, you take on the role of listener. Use validated hearing to understand and validate their responses. Listen carefully for them to voice their motivators. Validate what you heard by paraphrasing back to them your understanding of what they said.

Validated hearing involves three steps:

1. Paraphrase back your understanding of what you believe they said. Lead-ins might be: "Let me make sure I've got this" or "So, if I'm understanding you correctly."

2. Check for accuracy. Prove to them you heard them. Prove to yourself you heard and understood them. Lead-ins might include: "Did I get that right?" or "Am I understanding you?" Listen closely for information in these areas…

   • Their problem(s) or potential opportunity
   • If a problem, what is the cause of their problem

— 182 —

- Obstacles or challenges they're facing in trying to address their problem(s) or seize their opportunity
- Their desired situation
- Motivators
- Desired feelings
- Level of urgency
- Resolution concerns that might involve money, time, energy, effort

3. Prompt for more information.
   Only good things happen—only good things happen when you paraphrase back what you believe you heard, for example:

- The speaker verifies that you are correct or accurate. Excellent!
- They expand on their answer. They provide more information. Even better!
- They correct you if your paraphrase back was incorrect or inaccurate. While this may initially seem negative, it is actually one of the most important and positive things that can happen. This way the both of you take care of any misunderstanding or miscommunication right there and then. This will save each party a lot of time and frustration.

Their words—listen carefully to the words they use. Listen closely to detect emotions. As mentioned earlier, in the design and deliver steps, you will quote them. When presenting, use their *words* to validate their motivators. Then position how your offering will satisfy those motivators.

Feelings/state—People crave the feeling(s), the state they believe they'll experience by satisfying a motivator. To influence others, always communicate the feeling(s) your prospect will experience by satisfying their motivator. Each time you state a benefit of your offering, communicate the feelings the benefit will enable your prospective customer to experience. Throughout the presentation, communicate clearly and often the feelings they can expect.

To reiterate, what you learn and understand about their motivators and associated feelings will be an integral part of the design and delivery of your presentation.

Now that you've gathered this valuable intelligence, what do you do with it?

Your Expertise and Offering

What specific motivators can your expertise and offering address?

- What areas of existing pain can your expertise and offering help relieve?
- What areas of potential pain can your expertise and offering help avoid or eliminate?
- What areas of achieving gain can your expertise and offering help manifest?

What feelings will they experience when your solution satisfies their motivator(s)?

Create a comprehensive list of the motivators and feelings your expertise and offering can address. When presenting, skillfully tie their needs (using their words) to your offering. Obviously, the better the fit, the more likely the sale.

It is paramount that you communicate in a crystal-clear fashion the "what's in it for them" with every presented component of your offering.

Also, communicate how your offering will help them to relieve existing pain, avoid potential pain, or help them achieve gain. Back up your declarations with solid evidence.

And, make sure to ask for the sale. How will you ask? What words will you use? Decide on what works for you, rehearse it, and make it a very natural part of closing your presentation. These words should easily and confidently roll off your tongue. A couple examples: "Are you ready to move forward?" and "May I have your business?"

Not only is it what you say, but how you come across when you are interacting with the prospective customer. How do they perceive you? People like to do business with people they like. People do business with people they believe in.

Let's take a look at aspects of character in element three.

3: Trust + Credibility + Confidence

Trust, credibility, and confidence—these aspects of character must fill the relationship atmosphere. You must radiate trust, credibility, and confidence … at all times. People are convinced within. Conviction takes place within the emotional and logical core of the buyer. A presenter must influence conviction. The aspects of character that help influence conviction are paramount. These aspects of character must be ever present.

First and foremost, be a trustworthy, credible, and confident individual. Alas, it's not enough to *be* so. The prospective customer must *believe* you are so. Prospective customers are subconsciously deciding whether or not they believe you are trustworthy, credible, and confident. Their perception of you is their reality.

How do prospective customers determine whether or not you are trustworthy, credible, and confident? What determines their belief? These five areas influence their perception:

1. Your reputation—if they know or know *of* you. What IS your reputation?
2. Your understanding—by proving to them you *understand them* and *their situation*
3. Your presentation itself—the *content* of your presentation, what you say and what you show
4. Your appearance—how you *look* when you listen and speak
5. Your sound—how you *sound* when you speak

The Ultimate Sales Presentation^{sm} Mantra

When people are *convinced*, they will experience the *feeling(s)* they crave by *satisfying their motivator(s)*; they will take *action*.

Summary

In your business and personal life, there are multitudes of people longing to solve their problems, hoping to avoid potential problems, and aspiring to seize opportunities. The degree to which you can help people in these areas will determine your value to them. The degree to which you can effectively communicate this value will determine your success. When they associate worth to the value offered and are convinced of the feelings they will experience, they will invite you into their world. When they experience the value, they will invite you to stay. So…

Address their motivator(s). Thoroughly understand your prospective customer's motivator(s) and skillfully tie your solution to solving their existing or potential problems or helping them to seize opportunity.

Associate the feeling(s)/state. Clearly communicate the feelings/state they will experience by satisfying their motivators.

Influence their conviction. By radiating trust, credibility, confidence you win their hearts and minds. Clearly prove how your offering will address their motivators and lead them to experience their desired feelings. You accomplish this by designing focused and convincing presentations and delivering them with captivating excellence.

Lead them to yes.

My ask of you is that you apply what you've learned in this chapter. Make the lessons learned an integral, active part of your sales practice. Why? What's in it for you? An increased likelihood of receiving a yes.

Fill Your Heart with Confidence and Courage

People often ask, "How do I control my nerves when presenting?" First of all, be confident in knowing that by incorporating what you've learned in this chapter, you will be positioning yourself to succeed, which is a great confidence-builder.

In addition, prior to presenting, reduce your nerves by reciting, out loud and with conviction, the following, which I call "A Sales Presenter's Mindset":

> *These people are about to be WOW-ed.*
> *I am a good person who cares deeply about their well-being.*
> *I am prepared and thoroughly understand their motivators and desired feelings.*
> *I am going to introduce tremendous value today. Value they can use to better their lives.*
> *I am going to provide what they need to solve their problems and seize their opportunities.*
> *I am going to give them my very best.*
> *I am going to give them my heart and soul.*
> *Yes ... these people are about to be WOW-ed.*

Happy selling!

About the Author

Garry Terhune trains and coaches people who design and deliver sales presentations. He brings over 40 years of sales, sales training, and coaching experience to the global marketplace. He has successfully trained and coached thousands of individuals, both face-to-face and virtually, for many of the world's most prestigious organizations. He has loved every minute of it.

Garry trains and coaches his own programs: The Ultimate Sales Presentation℠ and The Ultimate *Virtual* Sales Presentation℠. Both programs focus on excelling in today's ever-changing and competitive marketplace where a thorough understanding of a prospective customer's situation is vital *a*nd where highly effective sales presentations are imperative to winning the business.

Garry always brings infectious energy and deep caring to each engagement. He is passionate about teaching and coaching sales and sales-support people because not only do the skills learned increase sales, they contribute to people's overall success, happiness, and well-being.

Email: garry@garryterhune.com
Website: www.garryterhune.com

CHAPTER TWENTY-TWO
SALES STARTS WITH—
"HOW CAN I SERVE?"

By Désirée van der Laan
Sales & Performance Coach and Trainer
Zürich, Switzerland

Approach each client with the idea of helping him or her to solve a
problem or to achieve a goal, not of selling a product or service.
—Brian Tracy

In my experience, I've learned that relying solely on sales structure won't make you a superstar. True success in sales comes from your personal journey. Flourish in sales by putting in unique efforts, staying resilient, and building genuine connections.

Embrace your strengths, overcome challenges, and serve like a pro. Your path to sales excellence is yours alone. By asking yourself, "How can I serve?" you'll surpass boundaries and form genuine connections.

Remember, your sales structure is a stepping stone, but you are the star. Your dedication and authenticity will truly elevate you. Now, let me share the most valuable methods I've observed in sales peak performers.

Step into the Realm of Sales Mastery: Where Clients Are More Than Just Numbers!

In my coaching experience, I've observed many individuals who become overwhelmed by the pressure to meet their targets, causing them to lose sight of the importance of genuinely connecting with their clients. As a result, they lose the joy and enthusiasm in their client interactions, turning it into a mere obligation. However, I firmly believe in the significance of bringing fun back into sales and truly relishing the conversations with your clients.

It's essential to remember that sales should not be a burdensome task but an opportunity for meaningful engagement. By approaching each interaction with a sense of enjoyment, you can create a positive and authentic connection with your clients. When you genuinely appreciate the conversations and the value you can provide, it becomes a source of fulfilment and satisfaction.

Let's shift the perspective and find joy in sales again. Let's make a conscious effort to infuse fun into every sales conversation. Rediscover the pleasure of connecting with your clients, building relationships based on trust, and finding innovative ways to meet their needs. By bringing back the joy, sales can once again become a rewarding and fulfilling experience for everyone involved.

A few years ago, I coached John, a sales representative who was feeling burnt out and disconnected from his clients. He realised that he had been solely focused on reaching his targets, often neglecting the genuine connection with his clients. Determined to find joy in his work again, John decided to embrace a service to sales mindset.

He started by actively listening to his clients, taking the time to understand their unique needs, challenges, and goals. Instead of pushing for quick sales, John aimed to provide exceptional service and personalised solutions that truly addressed his clients' pain points.

By going the extra mile and offering ongoing support, John forged deeper relationships with his clients. He discovered the immense satisfaction that comes from helping them overcome challenges and achieve their objectives. This not only exceeded his sales targets but also brought him a renewed sense of fulfilment and joy in his work.

As a result of his service-oriented approach, John's clients viewed him as a trusted advisor and valued partner. They were more likely to engage in long-term business relationships with him and enthusiastically referred him to others in their networks.

John's shift to a service-to-sales mindset not only revitalised his career but also brought him a renewed sense of purpose and joy in serving his clients. He became a top-performing sales representative who not only met his targets but also built lasting relationships based on trust and value.

As in the example of John, it is crucial to stand out from the crowd in today's competitive world. Just selling is not enough. Clients and even sales representatives yearn for a connection and with a „how to serve mindset" you can engage with your clients in exceptional ways, for example, understanding their needs, offering tailored solutions, and exploring opportunities for up-selling and cross-selling.

How Can You Improve Your Service-to-Sales Mindset?

To enhance your sales game and foster stronger client relationships, adopting a service-to-sales mindset is paramount. From my experience, the following three pillars—serve, engage, and focus—play a vital role in making this transformation happen.

The first pillar is serving the client's needs by taking a consultative approach. Leave behind the pushy salesperson persona and prioritise understanding your clients' businesses and challenges. Tailor your solutions to meet their specific needs, building trust and positioning yourself as a trusted advisor. By doing so, you'll forge stronger client relationships.

The second pillar emphasises meaningful engagement with potential clients. It's not about bombarding them with sales pitches; it's about displaying genuine interest in their businesses and goals. Ask open-ended questions and actively listen to their responses. Understanding their needs enables you to offer solutions that truly make a difference. Building rapport creates a relaxed atmosphere, leading to more fruitful conversations and positive outcomes.

The third pillar involves maintaining focus on the client's needs and goals throughout the sales process. This requires flexibility and adaptability. Be prepared to adjust your approach as their needs evolve. By doing so, you build trust, credibility, and increase the likelihood of closing more deals.

By embodying these three pillars, you'll not only witness improvements in your sales results but also cultivate stronger client relationships. Ultimately, this approach will contribute to your long-term success in sales.

Let's Dive a Bit Deeper Into the Three Pillars

Here's a real-life example of how adopting a service-to-sales mindset with the three pillars of serve, engage, and focus can lead to success.

When I coached Sarah, a sales rep for a software company, she'd been struggling to meet her sales targets and build strong relationships with clients. But then she decided to adopt a service-to-sales mindset and focus on the three pillars of serve, engage, and focus.

First, she took a consultative approach and prioritised serving the client's needs. She spent time listening to her clients and understanding their business challenges. Then she offered them tailored solutions that met their specific needs. For example, when a client mentioned that their employees were struggling with remote work, Sarah suggested software tools that could help them manage their tasks more efficiently. By doing so, she was able to build trust and establish herself as a trusted advisor. She truly developed an outward mindset.

Next, she engaged with potential clients in a meaningful way. Instead of bombarding them with sales pitches, she asked open-ended questions and really listened to what they had to say. By showing genuine interest in their business and goals, she built rapport and created a more relaxed atmosphere. This led to more fruitful conversations and better outcomes.

Finally, she stayed focused on the client's needs and goals throughout the sales process. When a client's needs changed, she was quick to adapt and suggest different solutions. And when a client faced a challenge with the software, she provided prompt and helpful support. By doing so, she built trust and credibility, and ultimately closed more deals.

Thanks to her adoption of a service-to-sales mindset with the three pillars of serve, engage, and focus, Sarah was able to improve her sales results, build stronger relationships with her clients, and achieve long-term success for herself and her company.

How Do You Develop a Serve Mindset?

Move away from a pure sales mindset and unleash the power of a serve mindset to transform your sales approach and build unbreakable client relationships. Check out these tips on how to cultivate a serve mindset:

- **Prioritise the client's needs.** Shift your focus from your own needs, wants, and goals to truly understanding your client's challenges, goals, and pain points. Listen actively, empathise, and offer tailored solutions that address their specific needs.

- **Be a problem solver and focus on the future.** Embrace the role of a problem solver rather than just a salesperson. Seek opportunities to add value to your clients' businesses and help them achieve their goals with your products or services.
- **Embrace honesty and transparency.** Transparency is key when adopting a serve mindset. Be honest about what your offerings can deliver and avoid making false promises. Guide clients with integrity, helping them make informed decisions.
- **Go the extra mile.** Stand out by going above and beyond for your clients. Provide exceptional client service, offer timely support, and be available to address their questions and concerns. Exceed their expectations consistently.
- **Cultivate long-term relationships.** View each interaction as an opportunity to build a long-term relationship. Stay connected with your clients, follow up after a sale, and continue to provide value and support beyond the initial transaction.

Yes, I know you've heard of these tips probably multiple times. Are you really understanding the importance of this? Out of my experience, we tend to be far ahead of the client and pitching our service already, without having the client onboard.

As Steven Covey, states in Steven Covey, states in *The Seven Habits of Highly Effective People*, „Seek first to understand, then to be understood."

How Do You Quickly Engage the Client?

Engaging a client quickly is essential to understanding the client, building a good relationship, and increasing your chances of making a sale. Here are some tips on how to quickly engage a client:

- **Unleash the power of open-ended questions.** Go beyond surface-level conversation and dive deep into the client's world. Ask open-ended questions that encourage them to share their thoughts and feelings. Follow up with clarifying questions to gain a comprehensive understanding of their needs and aspirations.

- **Activate your listening skills.** When the client speaks, be an active listener. Give your undivided attention, absorb their needs, goals, and challenges, and take notes to demonstrate your attentiveness. This not only helps you grasp what matters most to them but also shows your genuine appreciation for their input.
- **Infuse enthusiasm into the conversation.** Fuel the client's excitement by showing your genuine enthusiasm for their business and goals. Convey your passion for how your product or service can help them achieve their objectives. Let your energy be contagious, making them feel engaged and confident in the value you bring.
- **Paint vivid pictures with relevant examples.** Bring your offering to life by sharing compelling examples of how it has helped other clients accomplish their goals. Make these examples relevant to the client's industry or situation. This enables them to visualise the value your product or service can provide and reinforces their trust in your capabilities.
- **Master the art of concise communication.** Keep your engagement concise and to the point. Avoid overwhelming the client with technical terms or jargon they may not understand. Instead, use clear and simple language to effectively convey the benefits and unique selling points of your product or service.

I am sure you heard about these strategies multiple times. Unfortunately, I have seen different in various client conversations. Because we want to show we are the expert, keep control, and usually want to rescue our clients, we tend to fall into the "advice trap," and all of a sudden we forget about asking questions, do not listen to the client anymore, and give our pre-prepared solution. And we are still wondering why we did not make the sale. Well, guess what? The client did not feel listened to and understood.

If you want to increase your chances of winning, these are crucial tips that are often forgotten in the heat of a conversation.

How Do You Focus on What Is Important to the Client?

If you have focused on serving and engaging the client, the following tips are fairly easy to implement:

- **Prioritise the client's needs.** When you're engaging with the client, it's essential to prioritise their needs over your own. Focus on providing solutions that address their specific challenges and goals, and be willing to adapt your approach as needed.
- **Use their language.** To focus on what is important to the client, it's important to speak their language. Use terminology that they are familiar with, and avoid using technical jargon or acronyms that may be confusing.
- **Offer relevant solutions.** When you're presenting solutions to the client, make sure that they are relevant to their specific needs and goals. Avoid offering generic solutions that may not address their unique challenges.

Remember we were talking about painting the future? When focusing on the offering, this is crucial. The client should get the feeling they are understood, you are there to help solve their problems, and you are looking into a bright future. Tell it with a story that the client can relate to.

So how to get from a driven sales advice mindset to a real "how can I serve mindset"? As I mentioned in the very beginning, it is all about you and how much you practise. Self-awareness is the key to become a peak performer, not only in sales.

How Do You Peak Perform in Sales?

Maybe the following example resonates with you: early in my sales career, I made a common mistake that many salespeople make: I was so focused on making a sale that I overlooked my client's needs and concerns. I launched into my sales pitch with all the enthusiasm of a telemarketer on a caffeine high, spouting off technical jargon and industry buzzwords like there was no tomorrow. I thought I needed to show the client that I knew what I was talking about, as I often felt not taken seriously.

To my horror, my client looked at me like I was speaking gibberish. They didn't ask any questions, and I could tell they were completely disengaged. It was like I was trying to sell them a rocket ship, and they just wanted a bicycle. I realised that I had completely missed the mark and felt like a total idiot.

So, I took a step back and reflected on my approach to sales. I realised that I needed to serve my clients by truly understanding their needs and concerns.

I needed to engage with them on a personal level and find common ground to build rapport. I also needed to focus on the benefits of the service I was selling, rather than just the features.

The next time I met with my client, I tried a different tactic. I asked them about their weekend and what they liked to do for fun. And when it came time to explain the service's value, I used relatable analogies to help them understand how it could benefit them. I focused on how the service could help them achieve their goals and solve their problems.

Suddenly, my client's eyes lit up, and I could tell they were really engaged. They even shared their own experiences and concerns, which gave me valuable insight into how I could better serve them.

Long story short, my more personal and relatable approach paid off. I closed the sale, and my client was happy with their purchase. And as an added bonus, I learned that by serving and engaging with my clients, I could build lasting relationships and achieve long-term success in sales.

To Improve Your Sales, First Work on Yourself

Self-reflection is an essential practice that allows you to gain a better understanding of yourself and your performance. It's like looking in a mirror that reveals both your strengths and areas for improvement. Although it can feel challenging, especially in a dynamic and unpredictable field like sales, self-reflection helps you identify the roadblocks holding you back and develop strategies to overcome them. With self-reflection, you can celebrate your achievements, learn from your mistakes, and stay motivated to become the top performer in your sales career. So take a moment to reflect on your progress, assess your growth areas, and adjust your approach. It's the key to success and fulfilment in the exciting and constantly changing world of sales.

What Do You Do with All This Self-Reflection?

Despite my best intentions, I find it challenging to practice self-reflection daily. Time constraints, conflicting priorities, and unforeseen circumstances often hinder my ability to establish a consistent practice routine. However, I am determined to overcome these obstacles and make the most of the practice opportunities that do arise. I recognise that even small moments of focused practice can make a significant difference in my growth and progress.

By finding creative solutions, adjusting my schedule, and making practice a non-negotiable priority, I will gradually build a habit of regular practice and unlock the immense benefits it offers. I am committed to embracing the power of consistent practice, no matter the challenges that come my way.

Did you know that the time it takes to create a habit can vary depending on the individual and the specific habit being formed? According to research, it can take anywhere from 18 to 254 days to create a habit, with the average being around 66 days.

Here are some of my favourite tips for developing and maintaining a daily practice habit:

- **Start small and achievable.** Set realistic goals that can be accomplished in a short amount of time. Begin with small steps like asking one extra question a day or practising a specific sales technique for ten minutes.

- **Establish a routine.** Create a daily schedule that incorporates your practice habit. Whether it's dedicating the first 30 minutes of your morning or carving out time during your lunch break, find a consistent time slot that works for you.

- **Stay accountable.** Hold yourself accountable by tracking your progress, setting reminders, or sharing your goals with a colleague or mentor who can provide support and motivation.

- **Embrace imperfection.** Understand that daily practice is about progress, not perfection. Embrace mistakes as valuable learning opportunities and use setbacks as fuel for improvement. One day you are getting there, and the other day you are even worse. This belongs to the process of learning new habits.

- **Reflect and learn.** Take time to reflect on your client conversations, identify areas for improvement, and apply your learnings in future interactions. Consider keeping a journal to document your progress and celebrate your achievements.

- **Seek feedback.** Seek feedback from trusted mentors, peers, or experienced sales professionals. Embrace constructive criticism as a means to refine your skills and enhance your performance.

- **Celebrate milestones.** Acknowledge and celebrate your milestones and achievements along the way. This will boost your motivation and inspire you to keep pushing forward.

- **Connect with like-minded individuals.** Join communities or net-working groups where you can connect with other sales professionals. Engaging with like-minded individuals will provide valuable insights, support, and inspiration for your sales journey. Best practice is a key to getting better at what you do.

Remember, you have the power within you to become an exceptional per-former. Let your dedication, authenticity, and the insights shared here guide you on your path to peak sales mastery. Get ready to unleash your full potential and revolutionise your sales game!

Adopting a service-to-sales mindset that revolves around the three pillars of serve, engage, and focus can help you become a peak performer in the sales field. However, achieving mastery in sales requires more than just adopting a mindset. It involves consistent self-reflection and daily practice to refine your skills, experiment with new approaches, and learn from both yours and oth-ers' successes and failures. To support you in the process of becoming a peak performer, a coach can make the difference by providing personal guidance, honest feedback, expert strategies, and continuous support, enabling you to unlock your full potential.

About the Author

Désirée van der Laan is a successful sales and performance coach, trainer, and leader in one of the big four. She provides sales masterclasses for consultants and delivers coaching to individuals and teams who want to level up their sales skills, mindset, or performance.

Désirée has over 15 years of international experience in service and sales roles. She has worked with a variety of people from various levels inside com-panies—from client service agents to consultants to directors. Most of her time she supported and led global teams in improving their sales performance. She has experience in the service, hospitality, retail, and telecommunications industries.

For sales and performance coaching (team and individual), coach-the-coach, or corporate speaking, reach out to Désirée to connect.

LinkedIn: https://www.linkedin.com/in/desireevanderlaan/

CHAPTER TWENTY-THREE

CONQUER YOUR MIND, CONQUER YOUR LIFE

By Sandra Venere
Author, Wellness & Business Coach
Toronto, Ontario, Canada

The only limit to our realization of tomorrow will be our doubts of today.
—Franklin D. Roosevelt

In today's world, many of us strive to become the best we can be in all areas of our lives. Sometimes we forget that in order to become successful we must first and foremost conquer our mindset. Without that, we may have small successes along our journey but not enough to sustain and fulfill our deepest desires. The desire that fills that longing discontentment that resides in all of us. I want to help you achieve peak performance in sales.

Have you ever stopped and thought about what you truly believe you can achieve? We become so focused on the goal of selling ourselves and making sure we have all the knowledge possible on the industry we are in. We try our best each and every day to show up as that confident, well-spoken individual, ready to take on the world. Some days are better than others. We try to understand why we sometimes fail and sometimes succeed. Just to be confused as to why this does not stay consistent.

We can start by asking ourselves, "What do I truly think of myself? Do I believe I can achieve the goals I set for myself? Am I confident enough to reach my quota? Is there anything I need to clear before I can reach my sales targets?"

Many of us never go deeper to look at what our minds are telling us each and every day. Our mind is our biggest critic, it is the ego speaking to us, and it always wants to protect us. We need to catch the negative thoughts once they come up and cancel them right away before they sabotage our daily life.

I am speaking from firsthand experience. I too have been on this journey over the past few years to quiet my ego mind that keeps telling me that I am not good enough, I am not worthy enough, and I shouldn't trust myself, and that has me asking, "Why can't I do this?" It was until I asked myself the above questions and was truly authentic with my answers that I finally succeeded with taking the initiative to start my own online coaching business. I do know that in order to succeed at anything we need to believe we can trust ourselves and the journey that is presented to us along the way. If there are roadblocks that come up, we need to work on why we feel the way we feel about ourselves and the thoughts we think. Sometimes we do not realize that it is those thoughts that keep us stuck. Stuck in the hamster wheel, doing the same thing over and over again to only find ourselves in the same spot as we were from the start.

Unless we overcome those limited beliefs, we will never achieve peak performance in sales or most any other area. Overcoming limited beliefs is the first of many tools I'd like to share with you.

Tool #1—Limiting Beliefs

Look at your habits around the limiting beliefs. These habits are keeping you from achieving your full potential, both in sales and in other areas of your life. Make a list of your current habits that may be stifling you and keep you from achieving your dreams. These are the habits that you need to change the beliefs around. What are you telling yourself when you are engaging in these habits? This is the key to uncovering your beliefs. Once you are aware of the beliefs, you are then able to change them. This will then begin to uncover the mystery behind why the habits still exist.

Tool #2—Communication

Take small steps forward and this will start the process of success. For example: most sales positions require an open, communicative personality. If you find you lack this, then this is the next tool you need to work on. You may want to start conversations with people on your off-time at work. Start to realize that in order to sell yourself you need to be confident in who you are. Most of us lack the confidence we need to go to the next level. You may even want to take a short intensive course on communication skills. Another option would be to read books on how to communicate and influence people to trust and buy from you.

Tool #3—Repetition

Write down your sales goals. The act of writing these goals imprints into your subconscious mind the starting point of achieving the goals. Saying the goals out loud does not do the same, as we all seem to think it does. It has been proven that writing is the first step. Repetition is another tool to assist in making your goals come to fruition. You can start with a new journal page each morning and rewrite your goals and read them out loud, over and over again throughout the day. Read it like you believe it! "Conquer your mind, conquer your life." This will allow it to slowly become a habit. Once your habit becomes habitual is when you start seeing that your behavior is a resemblance of the goals you have written down. It is at this point where you will start to see that your behavior is starting to become your reality.

Tool #4—Desire

I recall when I was just beginning my journey of becoming a writer, I definitely wanted to become an author and write my first book. I did not know how or where to start. Even though I lacked the knowledge and the know-how to write a book, what I had was the strong desire to make this happen.

Without the strong desire to reach our goals and sales targets, we will never succeed. This is something that starts from within. A passion to reach your intended sales goals. I do know that you may be saying to yourself right now, "Do I have that passion? Is this something that I have seen before when I want to achieve something? Or am I striving for the impossible?" Let me tell you that if you are reading this book, you definitely are that person. You have the desire to achieve and have already taken the first action step to success by taking the initiative to seek out knowledge from a book.

Tool #5—Terror Barrier

Overcome the terror barrier. This means that halfway through your goal you begin to doubt yourself to the point where it freezes you in your tracks and does not allow you to continue to reach your goals. This happens to all of us at some point during our goal-setting challenges. We need to identify and avoid this barrier or it will sabotage our success. Review the goals you have set up for yourself and ask yourself, "Is this what I really want? Or is this what I am settling for?" If you knew you had the ability to succeed at all goals, what would that one major goal be? Would it be more than the initial goal you wrote down? If so, write out your new sales goals. If you find after writing that you have made a change in your goal and it is even more of a challenge, then you know you may have some fear behind the initial goal you wrote. By telling you to write out a goal where you know you will achieve it, this makes you less fearful. Now write down your fears that are linked towards getting your original goal and new goal. Once you have written down all your fears, you need to bust through this barrier and continue to realize that those fears are not real and do not serve you. They only keep you stuck. Stuck from achieving peak performance.

Your fear is not allowing you to see all the benefits that you will receive from achieving your goals. You need to turn your fears around. If you list all the possibilities that you will receive from achieving your goals, this will start to eliminate that barrier. Make a decision now that you are going to bust through this terror barrier and make sure it is real for you. Try to imagine yourself reaching your new goal and what that would feel like and look like. Using your imagination and visualization is another tool needed to succeed.

Tool #6—Visualization and Imagination

Visualization and imagination go hand in hand with each other and assist us in making our goals become a reality. The best way to utilize this tool to make it the most effective in reaching peak performance is to take the time each day to visualize your goal and your life. See yourself as the person you want to be, the one that believes in themselves, a great communicator, self-confident, and disciplined. When we visualize the life we want, we slowly move towards that life. By doing so we slowly develop a character that has a growth mindset as opposed to a fixed mindset. We need a growth mindset to become a peak performer in any area of our lives, sales and beyond.

Someone with a growth mindset views intelligence, abilities, and talents as learnable, and with conscious effort it will be achieved. On the other hand, someone with a fixed mindset views those same traits as unchangeable over time, and they get stuck in their own limiting beliefs. An example of a growth mindset is someone who wants to start their own business but does not know where to start, and they do not have any education on where to begin. Instead of thinking the negative thought, "I cannot do this without being educated," they see it as a challenge and a learning opportunity.

When you have a growth mindset, you believe you can gain the knowledge and skills necessary to succeed. Given the numerous challenges that entrepreneurs face, this type of mindset will lead you to become successful and achieve peak performance.

Tool #7—Attitude

Your attitude will dictate where you go in life. It is the foundation of failure or success. Your attitude is a combination of your thoughts, your feelings, and your actions. This combination is what generates your energy. Your energy in turn sends out a vibration into the world. Whatever you send out into the world comes back to you. We tend to diffuse our energy and make excuses as to why we feel the way we do. The stories we make up so we do not have to succeed in any area of our life become our life. In order to change our attitude, we need to see how important it is in every life circumstance. Every circumstance has good and bad in it. The big question is—what do you look for? That is going to dictate your attitude. There is no right way to do anything. It can be a good or valid way, but clearly understand there is always a better way. And with the right attitude you will find it. This is why attitude is very important when trying to achieve peak performance in any area of your life.

After taking the time to see a current situation in a completely different (positive) scenario, you can begin to change your attitude towards it. When you change your attitude, the situation will begin to change. Now ask yourself this question—how important is attitude?

Tool #8—Action

Once you compile all the above tools and begin to notice a change within, it is now time to take action. If you are currently in a sales position, then I suggest you try using these tools on your next sales pitch or customer. Once you do, you can then reevaluate how the sale went. Did you find that the techniques helped you close the sale more easily than what you are used to? Did you find it was easier to communicate? If you answered yes to these questions, then this is a good sign that you implemented the tools correctly.

Another option you can do is to continue to take action steps with your visualization and imagination. This exercise is a critical component to the outcome of your success. I would say that if you can continue on a daily basis to use this tool, you will begin to see a dramatic change. Keep focusing on the result. Picture yourself achieving that sales goal.

Another action you can take that is very important and that aligns with the above is tool 3, repetition. Continue to journal and write out your goals, and be as specific as you can with each goal. Read what you write every day, as much as you can. You can place sticky notes on your computer, mirror, and anywhere that you spend most of your time in. This will help assist you because as you see the notes, you will read the message and it will imprint in your mind. There is something to be said when it comes to reprogramming our mind, and repetition is key.

Tool #9—Responsibility

An absolute prerequisite for success in every aspect of your life is responsibility. Responsibility for your successes and failures. With every success there is victory, and with every failure there is a learning lesson. Individuals who do not take responsibility for their actions waste their full potential. Make certain you are not in this category. You have so much more potential than you can imagine.

Poor people have become millionaires, uneducated farmers have solved world problems. Anything is possible if you continue to persist and know how to get the most out of yourself. You do that by taking responsibility for your life. There is no one out there that is going to do your work for you. You have to remember that it is always your responsibility to go after what you want in life. It all begins with you.

You can ask someone for help or hire a mentor or coach, but in the end, they are not going to do the work for you. They will be there to guide you in the right direction. To stop you when you may be making the wrong choices. The quicker you learn the above tools, the sooner you will build the confidence that no matter what, you have your own back when it comes to life itself.

I recall a time when I was really unsure about all the decisions I was making in life, whether it be my relationships, work, friends, and family. I had to acquire knowledge and tools so that I could get where I am now—helping others. It did not happen overnight. It took a lot of personal development work as well as taking a leap of faith and conquering my fears.

I truly believe that if you have the desire, the rest comes naturally. The desire and belief go hand in hand. If you do not believe you can, you won't. This is why we need to look back at the old stories we tell ourselves and know that they are not real. They came to us throughout life from our parents, caregivers, friends, family, and teachers. They made an impression on us because we were young and needed to learn from them. It does not mean that these stories were stories we should continue to believe about ourselves. Once we acknowledge this, an entire world of opportunities exists for us to explore. What a beautiful life we can now create for ourselves. You can begin to see yourself reaching all your sales quotas, goals, and dreams.

Never give up on yourself, keep striving each day to take small steps to get closer to your goals. Also remember that our language has a lot to do with our outcomes in life. There are a host of words in our language that we should concentrate on eliminating from our daily thoughts. Words like "can't," "impossible," and "hopeless." They carry a negative connotation that will work against our success. Also, we have to be careful with the words and thoughts we think. Although we often do not realize this, the thoughts we think actually bring about the very thing we do not want to happen.

There is another reason why we may tend to doubt ourselves, and that is because we lack self-confidence, self-esteem, or both. This hinders our success in anything we do. Self-confidence grows with successful accomplishments, even if only small ones, building one on top of another. Eventually you will become that confident person you were born to be.

With this confidence you can reach your peak performance in sales, you will keep growing to new levels, and you will see how all these tools have helped mold you into the person you were always meant to become.

About the Author

Sandra Venere is the author of *7 Keys to Unlock Your Dream Life*. She is a wellness and business coach, and she has her own online coaching business where she helps people discover their vision and helps them make choices that lead them to their goals and dreams. She also created a digital course called Unlock Your True Potential, which you can find on her website.

Sandra ran a business with her brother in the beauty industry, which is now a global company. She worked in many areas of the business while also receiving her license as a nutritionist and personal trainer. She studied online at Seneca College and received two certifications, one in psychology and one in finance.

With all that Sandra has done up to this point she truly believes that it is the power of the mind and controlling what we believe and think that leads us to failure or success. She has always loved to help people, whether it be through listening, giving sound advice, or lending a helping hand. She knew that she had to turn all her life journeys into books of knowledge and wisdom from firsthand experience. She will be working on her next book in the near future, a book dedicated to helping people overcome their obstacles in life and come out of it with more wisdom and grace.

Email: Sandra.venere1234@gmail.com
Website: www.sandravenere.ca

CHAPTER TWENTY-FOUR
GIVING UP IS NOT AN OPTION

By Amy Schmidt Wullenweber
Business Executive, Health & Wellness Coach
Cincinnati, Ohio

The difference between a successful person and others is not a lack
of strength, not a lack of knowledge, but rather a lack of will.
—Vince Lombardi

As a young girl, I was painfully shy and soft spoken. I absolutely hated being the center of attention. I have a vivid memory of an evening we went out to celebrate one of our birthdays—for special occasions we would eat dinner at the country club. I may have been seven years old at the time. I never liked to order for myself at the club because we were always seated at a round table and all eyes would be fixed on whoever was ordering.

When it was my turn to order, I started to talk, but the waiter could not hear me. I had not yet mastered the skill of projecting my soft-spoken voice, so he asked me to repeat myself. I could feel my face turn bright red and I looked over at my sister who was snickering at me. The embarrassment took over and I could not hold back my tears. I excused myself from the table and ran to hide in the bathroom, hoping no one would notice I was gone.

That is just one of many scenarios from my childhood that would have indicated a career in sales was not in my future. Circumstances eventually changed when I was going into my adolescent years after my parents' divorce and subsequent move to the other side of the city. It was then that I learned to

— 207 —

push myself out of my comfort zone. I met many new friends, who also turned out to be life-long friends. This early life experience served me well and by the time I was a teenager I definitely found my voice—times ten.

In our society, we have this preconceived notion of certain personality traits top-performing salespeople might have. A few that come to mind are extrovert, gregarious, and pushy. They do whatever it takes to win. While I do not disagree with that notion entirely, I'd be remiss not to point out that some of the most talented sales executives with whom I have worked did not possess those qualities.

One memory from early on in my career that exemplifies this is from when I was still in training and needed to shadow some of the more experienced reps during their sales calls. The two top-performing reps, who each consistently exceeded their goals every quarter, could not have been more different in their personalities. One was blessed with the gift of gab and did not know a stranger anywhere she went. The other was more reserved and thoughtful when he spoke, making every person in the room feel seen and heard. It was eye-opening for me at the time when I realized their comparable success had nothing to do with their personality traits.

For any salesperson to reach their peak performance level, it has to start with a solid foundation of motivation and drive to succeed. If the inherent desire to push yourself is not there, then you are not likely going to be breaking records anytime soon. Top performers are usually not any more talented than their peers, they are just more committed to do their best every day. They take the time to plan out their work weeks and days, carving out time for tasks that they know are necessary to get ahead. They do the work because it needs to be done, not necessarily because they love it, and they always show up prepared.

Perseverance

In April 2020, in the midst of the global pandemic, I joined the millions of other professionals who were laid off from their jobs. I had another setback a few months later in August 2020 when I received the shocking news that I had breast cancer. Looking back on that experience still feels very surreal. Our world had completely shut down, which was strange enough, and then, seemingly out of nowhere, I had cancer. My treatment plan was to include two major surgeries, six months of chemo, and four weeks of radiation. Mentally, I was preparing for battle, and physically, I was gearing up for the "marathon" of my life.

Over the next ten months that followed my diagnosis, I did what I needed to do to get through it. Since I wasn't working at the time, the only thing that made me feel somewhat normal was to exercise. I planned my (at home) workouts to fall on the three days of the week I would feel best. The other four days were spent resting and recovering from the effects of the chemo. I had worked up to the highest intensity workout prior to my diagnosis, and I was determined to not let cancer take away my physical strength. My goal during treatments was to do the entire one-hour workout, start to finish, three times per week. Even when the cumulative effects of chemo started to take over and I became so anemic that walking up a flight of stairs was challenging, I pushed myself every week to get those three workouts in. Some days it took me two and a half hours to get through, but the only thing that I mattered was that I finished.

Shortly after my cancer war ended, I was eager to get back to work and transition back to "civilian" life. Entering the workforce again after beating cancer was also a formidable experience. After a disheartening career misstep, I took some time to stop and really think about what this next chapter would look like for me. I was even more determined to find an opportunity that would not take away from my life as a mom and wife, but instead to actually compliment it. The most important job I will ever have is to be a mother to my three amazing kids, and I will never again allow any job to compromise that. My determination to not settle ended up paying off, and I secured a position where my earnings potential would far surpass any previous earnings.

Confucius said, "It does not matter how slowly you go so long as you do not stop." The key words in that quote being, "so long as you do not stop." In sales, and in life, we will all experience setbacks at some point. It is inevitable. The setbacks, sometimes referred to as failures, are not as important as how we react to them. Top performers all have these things in common: they assess the situation, make adjustments to the plan, and take corrective action to keep moving forward towards their goal. That is how the term "fail forward," coined by John C. Maxwell, originated. In today's world, the word "failure" no longer has a negative connotation, which is considerably a good thing. However, if we learn to address setbacks with a positive mindset, they don't ever really have to become a failure. When I think of the word "failure," I think of giving up, throwing in the towel, and moving on to something different. It is the failure to keep trying.

As soon as we stop moving, we lose momentum. Persevering through obstacles and setbacks is what sets top performers apart from their peers. That said, it's important to point out that perseverance can mean something different for everyone at different times in their lives. After all, not all setbacks are created equal. Whether it is an illness, injury, financial loss, loss of a family member, divorce, loss of a job, etc., just surviving another day is perseverance for some people. To keep breathing in and out, one hour to the next, one day to the next, one week to the next—that is also perseverance.

Expect setbacks and plan accordingly. Top-performing clients with whom you have developed great relationships do suddenly slam on the brakes and say they are moving in a different direction. Key contacts move on to different roles, leaving you to have to start back at square one. Committing to keeping your pipeline healthy and robust is one way to offset these uncontrollables. Many companies will invest in a third party to help with lead generation for their sales team. While that may be enough for maintaining the status quo, top performers see it as more of a supplement to their own efforts to build their pipeline. Carving out time for prospecting is a priority and committing to doing it is imperative.

To stay focused on important tasks, like qualifying leads and prospecting, I schedule two-hour time blocks each day to only do those two things. Challenge yourself to see how much you can accomplish in those two hours and try to beat it the next time. The grind of making calls, sending emails, and calling again can be monotonous, so rewarding yourself with breaks can help keep you energized. During a break I might listen to a five-minute meditation or just get up and move around to get my blood flowing again.

I don't know many people who can honestly say they love cold calling. But when you really think about what prospecting is, it is not cold calling. I like to think of it more as fact-finding. You may talk to six different people within a company before you find out who the decision maker is. And then, just when you find out who the decision maker is, she tells you she is leaving and her replacement won't be hired for a few months. If you have done your job well, you may not need to completely start over. Turning a prospect into a client requires showing up to every call and establishing rapport with any contacts who could potentially be your allies.

On a curious note, have you ever been completely caught off-guard by a salesperson because they said something silly, made you laugh, and completely disarmed you from wanting to hang up or walk away? How does it feel when you walk away feeling a little lighter because another human being made you laugh? That is the mindset you want to get yourself in when you are prospecting.

Goal Setting and Discipline

I am and always have been an exercise enthusiast. I can remember back in the days of VHS tapes when the Jane Fonda workouts first were released. The challenge of the workout and exhilaration that followed after finishing it were euphoric. As soon as I was old enough to get a gym membership, I did. I was there religiously three days a week. I set nutritional goals for myself, kept track of my progress, and enjoyed measuring my success—and at times, setbacks.

During my years as a health coach, I spent a lot of time working on goal setting with my clients. The important thing about setting goals is that they need to be achievable. Doing a baseline assessment and defining a desired end result are critical to the success of not only achieving the first goal, but also keeping the momentum going and continuing to set higher goals. You start where you are and you build upon that. As you get stronger, you add more weight, more distance, and more intensity. Writing your goals down and setting deadlines for yourself will help keep you accountable and also build your confidence as you start achieving your goals.

The skills I developed earlier in life easily transferred over to my career in sales and certainly led to my success. In sales, your performance is measured against goals that have been set for you. Compensation plans and incentives are designed with those performance goals in mind. Top performers go a few steps further and set their own daily performance goals to work towards. They also ask for referrals from existing clients and know how to network and use social media to their benefit. Whether it be increasing your outreach efforts to prospects or aiming for a certain number of in-person meetings each week, it takes discipline to stay the course and to keep striving to achieve your peak performance.

Mind, Body, Spirit Alignment

I was baptized and raised in the Catholic faith. For many years after my parents' divorce, my mom felt ashamed and unwelcome in the Catholic Church. It didn't take long before our Mass attendance dwindled down to mostly just going on Easter and Christmas. I was so busy navigating the hills and valleys of being a teenager that I had no awareness of the gaping hole that was growing deep inside my soul. I was invincible—or so I thought.

By the time I was a freshman in college, it's safe to say I had lost any connection I once had with my faith. A traumatic experience that happened when I was 19 threw me into a tailspin from which I almost did not recover. I learned how to compartmentalize the residual pain from that trauma and was able to, by all outward appearances, function normally and do what needed to be done to finish college and earn my degree. I was so good at wearing that mask in social situations that no one would've ever suspected the extent to which I was struggling. The burden did eventually become too heavy to bear alone, and I believe it is God who placed some very special friends in my path during that time. God revealed Himself to me through those friends, and I am eternally grateful for that gift.

Upon graduating from college, I was the chosen recipient of a very prestigious award that took me on the greatest adventure of my life. The timing of it was perfect on so many levels.

Whether you believe in a higher power or not, I think this experience could still resonate with you. We go to great lengths to take care of our minds and our bodies, continually learning and striving for success, both mentally and physically. Why does it seem our emotional and spiritual health is the first to drop to the bottom of our priorities? It wasn't until I recognized my spiritual life was on empty and I surrendered and allowed God to fill back in that hole that I was once again able to see all the blessings I have been given and find true joy in my life.

Our minds, our bodies, and our spirits are all working together, and if they are not in sync with one another, chaos will likely ensue. This realization was pivotal in changing the direction I was headed and profound in leading me to opportunities that later presented themselves. During a recent night out to dinner with my husband, I announced with conviction that I was finally ready to start writing my book. The very next day, Erik reached out to me and asked if I would be interested in co-authoring the final book in his Peak Performance series. Coincidence? Maybe. But what if it wasn't?

The law of attraction is a simple one: visualize it, imagine it, and be open to receiving it. Could this idea of putting out in the universe that which we want and the universe providing be the real deal? Or could it just be that when we are open to new opportunities and brave enough to say yes, that more opportunities will unfold before us as a result? These are the same questions I am sure you have also pondered at one time or another while forming your own opinions that make the most sense to you and your belief system.

An older and much wiser friend once suggested to me that we are all just spiritual beings having a human experience. Thinking about this idea really resonates with me. Practicing yoga, meditating, making time for prayer, writing in a journal—these are all things you can do to start connecting to your spiritual self and your higher power. And be sure to prepare yourself for all of the great things that lie ahead in your sales career and in your life.

About the Author

Amy Schmidt Wullenweber is a tenured business development executive, culminating 20-plus years of sales success that spans several industries. A graduate from the University of Cincinnati, Amy earned her BFA in electronic media through the College-Conservatory of Music. She was also selected as the first recipient of the Procter & Gamble International Student Exchange award and spent several months studying and working in Munich, Germany.

Amy's passion to help others was ignited during her years working in pharmaceutical sales. While her children were young, Amy built her business as a health and wellness coach. Working with her clients and walking alongside them on their health journeys was transformative. She credits those years as an entrepreneur for taking her success in sales to the next level.

Amy is also a breast cancer thriver and has shared her story in a podcast interview, which is linked below. She plans to continue efforts to raise awareness as time allows.

Email: awullenweber@gmail.com
Website: https://podcasts.apple.com/us/podcast/asking-for-a-friend/
id1620788625?i=1000565279899

DID YOU ENJOY THIS BOOK?

If you enjoyed reading this book, you can help by suggesting it to someone else you think might like it, and **please leave a positive review** wherever you purchased it. This does a lot in helping others find the book. We thank you in advance for taking a few moments to do this.

THANK YOU

If you enjoyed reading this book, don't miss the other books in the Peak Performance Series:

Peak Performance: Mindset Tools for Leaders

Peak Performance: Mindset Tools for Business

Peak Performance: Mindset Tools for Entrepreneurs

Peak Performance: Mindset Tools for Athletes

You might also like other Thin Leaf Press titles:

Winning Mindset: Elite Strategies for Peak Performance

Winner's Mindset: Peak Performance Strategies for Success

The Successful Mind: Tools to Living a Purposeful, Productive, and Happy Life

The Successful Body: Using Fitness, Nutrition, and Mindset to Live Better

The Successful Spirit: Top Performers Share Secrets to a Winning Mindset

Ordinary to Extraordinary

Explore.

Printed in Great Britain
by Amazon

31129656R00136